Rabbinic Stories for the Christian Soul

Gilbert Press, Vallonia, Indiana

Library of Congress Cataloging-in-Publication Data (pending)

Rabbinic Stories for the Christian Soul / by Christopher G. Criminger.

     p.   cm.
Includes bibliographical references.
ISBN-13 9781466285699 ISBN-10: 1466285699
1. Christianity   2. Judaism   3. Christianity and other religions…

To my DAD,
Frederick O. Criminger,
who taught me the way of Christ
and to ask hard questions.

Contents

❈ | Foreword

There are many spiritual journeys people are on where God is showing His children new insights into life and God's Word. I have read many of the great mystical classics and loved the dessert fathers and the spiritual wisdom I gleaned from them. But when I started studying the Jewish roots of the Christian faith and discovered rabbinic tales and stories, I was amazed at their beauty and simplicity. Here was a spiritually powerful and rich religious tradition that falls in line with the Jewish tradition of the Bible but has either been ignored or forgotten some how.

I realized some Christians were doing experiments in their Christian faith like trying to live by all the Levitical laws of the Hebrew Bible to what one man referred to as "the year of living biblically." One church preached and tried to live out God's laws in radical ways in their community for a year.

As a Christian minister, I was always taught to have the Bible in one hand and the newspaper in the other. Why this was so important and relevant has escaped me over the years of seeing so many ministers driven more by contemporary issues than the burning issues within the Scriptures themselves. So here is the experiment I tried. I read the Bible in one hand and I read the Talmud in the other. I was utterly amazed at how these books were not contradictory but actually complementary to each other. I found so many similarities and parallels that the differences and contrasts were the exception rather than the rule.

Every chapter begins with a rabbinic story and many of them also end with one. Pastors and Christian teachers will find the rabbinic stories alone to be very portable and user-friendly. Christians who like theology and how the two testaments weave together like a wonderful mosaic may be interested in how these two streams of Jewish faith intersect and cross paths.

Any mistakes or weaknesses within this work are solely my own. I am grateful for the invaluable insights and editing that Scott Erwin has done on this project. The time and hours Scott has put into this work has been invaluable. I also want to thank Chris Hvezda for his encouragement and persistence in keeping me on track in finishing this book, as well as his help in the final phase of processing and packaging the manuscript for print. This work included his cover design..

I am especially thankful for the love and patience of my beautiful wife Sandy of twenty-five years of marriage. Her support and encouragement continues to keep me looking up when I am tempted to look down. And my four wonderful children continue to teach me what it means to be a follower of Jesus within the context of my own family. Tiffany and Tabitha are my two college girls and my two boys rule this year at school. My oldest son Craig is a senior in High School this year and my youngest son Kent is in the eighth grade in Middle School. God uses my family in so many indescribable ways that I am always humbled and honored by those who know me and love me best.

Preface

I have been on a long, slow journey back to the Jewish roots of the Christian faith. I spent many years reading books, listening to recordings of Christian speakers, and prayerfully "chasing" after God. I have been filled with the grandeur of wonder, reading the lives and biographies of the early Church Fathers, the great Catholic mystics, and the spiritual biographies of God's misfits and missionaries.

I grew up in the Baptist tradition and learned of the great martyrs in the Anabaptist tradition. I have served in a federation of churches that traces its roots back to the great Cane Ridge Revival that raged across the Midwest prairies of America.[1] Yet my heart longed for something long forgotten from the past as it hungered for God's great restoration of the future. My spirit soared with daring thoughts and burning songs, searching for signs and markers on this faith journey of life.

I have wrestled with God for a blessing for knowledge and wisdom only to limp away with the blessing seemingly just outside of my reach. So I got lost in the whirlwind of my own knowledge about God produced by a world and churches solely focused on passing fads and phases. Why is it so easy to tame and domesticate God by our own short sightedness while what is just beyond one's sight is where the real secret wisdom and horizon of God's knowledge resides?

I have been a "resident alien" in a church in exile for all my life. How can one be content when you know you are made for another world? How can one be satisfied with a church in ruins and fragmented beyond recognition? How can the world see Jesus in a church full of people who seem as lost and drifting aimlessly as others in the world are? The end of the age is coming to a close and God's preparation time is almost over. God is desiring to restore a unified witness of Israel and the church together so that the world will know and see God's *shekinah* glory in and within His people.

It seems the harder one strives, the more illusive the goal. Yet all this began to change when I attended the first clergy Promise Keepers in Atlanta Georgia. Bill McCartney, who pioneered Promise Keepers, said this event was the greatest move of God he had ever witnessed. Fifty thousand clergymen from every tribe and ethnic group were present. The theme was "racial reconciliation" and I did not have any idea the changes God was going to bring within my own life after this epiphany and awakening that happened in my inner-most spirit.

Max Lucado had just given a powerful message on church unity and Steve Green came and spontaneously led us in a heavenly moment of worship. All the various ethnic ministers came down in the thousands representing the many wounded and marginalized people of America's many diverse ethnic groups. Native Americans came and we cheered them on and high-fived them and showered them with all the love and encouragement we could muster. African Americans, Asians, Caribbean, Korean, even the handicapped came one, came all. Every nation and tribe came and there seemed to be no end to the long procession of people groups.

In the middle of voices filled with praise and tears came the Messianic clergy. Many Hasidic Jews wearing their black garments and black hats strolled down the aisles by the hundreds. Suddenly it happened… Across the giant stadium time seemed to stop. There was one Hasidic Messianic Jew walking and staring at me as I was solely focused upon him. I found myself walking toward him as if I was being pushed along by an invisible force. I had no idea what was happening nor what I was doing? When we met together on the floor, we embraced and held each other for a long time. There was such a large floodgate of emotion released from us that there were no tears left to cry when we were done.

All the while I did not really even know why or what was happening but when I looked into the window of this man's soul through his eyes, suddenly like a flash it was clear. Here I was a blond, blue eyed German American asking forgiveness for what the German people did to the Jews. Here was a "Christian-Messianic Jew" forgiving the German people for all the evil done to the Jewish people.

Since that Promise Keepers event, nothing has been the same. When I pray, I pray for peace upon Jerusalem and the safety of Israel. When I read the Scriptures, I suddenly find myself reading them with new eyes. I no longer read the Bible simply as a Gentile but as a spiritual Semite. I no longer read the Bible as I was taught in Bible College and Seminary, that the church had replaced Israel, but now for the first time

I understood the church is grafted "into" Israel and is "with" Israel.

A burning question today is, "Can the church reclaim its Jewish roots?" However people read the history of the first four centuries of the church, a huge change occurred between an almost totally Jewish church of the first century (Acts 1–9) and the church of the fourth century that required Jewish converts to renounce their Jewish identify and cease Jewish customs and observances.

If churches are going to deal with the scandal of division, it will only happen by looking at the first division that happened between Israel and the Church. It is only by going back that the church will be able to move forward in her destiny with Israel. It is only a matter of time till both Israel's and the church's destiny will climax together by the Messiah who resurrects and restores the broken-hearted and heals the wounded and reconciles the whole world to a new creation.[2]

The Talmud is the standard commentary of Jewish writings on Holy Scripture. The early church along with rabbinical Judaism grew and developed together at the same time. They both interpreted the Scriptures that reveal both continuity and discontinuity, particularly intersections that even show mutual influence and interdependence within their distinct groups. This study will not focus on the differences but the similarities between the Talmud and the Bible. It is at the intersections that their paths cross together as Messianic communities where the future restoration of Israel and the church dance together on the edge of destiny. The dance has already begun as many Jews and Christians discover together that only the Messiah can restore that which has been lost and heal that which has been broken and torn apart.

When one compares the Talmud with the Christian scriptures, one may ask why these books should be studied together. There are some incredible parallels and overlaps to be taken into consideration. First, both rabbinic Judaism and Christianity are Messianic movements. Second, both were mothered and nurtured by what I call "older Judaism," since both rabbinic Judaism and Christianity developed from the form of Judaism we encounter in the Hebrew Bible. Third, both were oral traditions that were later written down. The canonization process (accepting a collection of books for the Bible), whether the New(er) Testament or the Talmud, developed during the same historical period: between the second and fourth centuries. And last, both traditions are bound by Scripture and give important interpretive insights into God's Holy Word.

This renewed appeal to "origins" or "return" to the Jewish roots of the Christian faith is neither a reacquisition of early church primitivism nor an effort to recapture some pristine, pure Apostolic early church. It is rather a rediscovering and looking at the past and seeing something new that was not seen before. The whole history of the church has been one of establishment, corruption, renewal, retrieval, and revival. The scandal of division and the deep, continual fragmentation of churches can only be understood and repaired by a reexamination of the origins of Christianity and the promised restoration of Israel as God's chosen people.[3]

Introduction: Beginning *the* Story

A Jewish folktale finds God trying to determine who His chosen people will be. He first interviews the Greeks, asking them, "What could you do for me?" The Greeks promise God the finest art and the loftiest thinking. Then He interviews the Romans, who promise great buildings and wonderful road systems. After traveling around the world, interviewing one nation after another, He interviews a small Middle Eastern group. "Lord God," the Jewish people respond, "we aren't known for our art or power or roads. However, we are a nation of storytellers. If You were to be our God, and we were to be Your people, we could tell Your story throughout the world." "It's a deal!" says God, and the rest is "His-story."

Some people feel intellectually assaulted by the fact that God would choose a nation like Israel. They often view it as some kind of favoritism or unfairness. It's interesting that even the Talmud deals with this issue: "The selection of Israel was no arbitrary choice, and to avoid the imputation of favouritism to God… the Torah was offered to all the nations, but Israel alone agreed to accept it."[1] There are also some false ideas about Israel, like its election means a privileged status before God. It is true, we read in Holy Scripture of God's undying love and commitment to Israel, but we also read God's love and divine purpose for all the nations.[2]

As the story in Scripture unfolds, one begins to see that Israel's "chosen-ness" means not so much privilege as suffering, reproach, and humiliation, as Israel embodies God's own agony over a sin-filled, disobedient world. Christians to this day have fallen into the same trap as ancient Israel, thinking at times they have a claim on God's love which others do not have. The church sometimes forgets to read Paul's strong words, "there is no distinction between Jew and Greek; the same Lord is

Lord of all and bestows His riches upon all who call upon Him" (Rom. 10:12). God's grace, love, and truth are always embodied in a community made up of Jews and Gentiles, who are both called to be witnesses and bearers of God's love for all people.

We see in the history of Israel a nation divided into northern and southern kingdoms (1Kg. 12), as well as the people being scattered and going into exile. The Assyrian and Babylonian captivities were so cruel and corrosive to God's people that many of the prophets speak of a latter "day" when Israel will be vindicated and restored as a nation.[3] This promise of restoration is a visible expression of God's mercy (*hesed*) overcoming the internal divisions, sinfulness, and unfaithfulness of Israel. This kind of divine shattering and hardening of Israel lasts until, in Ezekiel's terms, the restoration of Israel occurs with their return as a united body (Eze. 39:25–29).

There are many parallels in the Church and churches today that are both so divided and scattered across the face of the earth. Israel represents a model for the Church's own exile and restoration. What I am suggesting, quite bluntly, is for Christians to read the Scriptures once again in a manner parallel to that of the first century Jewish believers. The credibility of the gospel story hinges on the very well-being and unity of God's Church.

The history of Israel is part and parcel of Christian history. Martin Buber wrote, "One is no longer a true Jew who does not himself remember that God led him out of Egypt."[4] God's story in Israel is "our" story, whether Jew or Christian in understanding one's election, hopes, failures, and destiny. One must either start reading the Scriptures as a Jew or maybe one should stop reading the Bible. But what does it mean to be spiritually a Jew? Certainly neither birth nor residence determines spiritual truth. Judaism and Christianity are about a way of life according to Torah; in other words, it describes a certain lifestyle, it describes people in a covenant relationship with the one, true, living God.

Of course our modern problem is aptly illustrated by a bumper sticker that provocatively reads, "Jesus, save us from Your followers." Others cannot see this Jesus clearly if the Church of Jesus Christ does not embody the Scriptures and providential unity to bring coherence and God's *shalom* in its own life. A more radical view of the Church along the lines of Rabbi Jesus would be a church as a visible community, like Israel in line with the entire history of the Church in union with the global community of Christians that make up all nations today.[5]

What God desires today is a united people, "Israel-with-the-Church," as God pours forth His Spirit in bringing all nations together under the Lordship of the Messiah King Yeshua/Jesus. The church at large must first let go of its political and material structures, cultural captivity and self-justifications. Going back to the beginning again, the church holds all things in common and has the same mind with all of God's people. A repentant and chastised church God will not reject.

The question cannot simply be the old one of "Where is the true Church?" It must now be, "What is God doing in the Church and how am I entering into that place of service and love?"[6] Humility, repentance, compassion, and restoration are the calling cards of the day as it has been throughout Church history. As we look at how history and Scripture unfold under the providence of God, we begin to see more clearly God's movements by which He uses nations to mold humanity into one new humanity in Christ with Jewish Israel. Discerning this unfolding history may be the Church and Israel's greatest challenge.

All the Bible is the story of how all of history is God's story. With veiled sight and hidden mysteries, people may miss this great defining story of life. But God has always had a people who have shared His story down through history. Some were tortured, jeered at, flogged, stoned, persecuted, mistreated, and even killed. The world was not worthy of them (Heb. 11:32–38). But God has planned something better for us (the Church) so that they (Israel) should not be made perfect apart from us (Heb. 11:40).

As one looks at history, one begins to see how the Church's and Israel's story have intersected, crossed paths many times as both are looking toward the culmination of all of history becoming "God's grand narrative." God's Word breaks forth in power and in story. God's story is the greatest story ever told. I love the story of a crippled old man who asked a Rabbi to tell him a story:

> *The rabbi told him a story of fear-filling grandeur and beauty, of vindication and the wonder of the eternal. When he was done, the old man leaped to his feet and began to dance and left shouting the praises of God. Now that is the way to tell a story!*

The Glory *of* Israel's Story

The Glory *of* God

A man asked a Rabbi where he might go to meet God. The Rabbi explained to him that he went up to a certain village to pray and meet with God. The next day, the man went up to that village and stood before a great mountain and cried out, "God, if You are real, show Yourself!" And when he received no answer, he cried out again and again and again but still there was no answer. Finally after many repeated attempts he finally gave up and declared, "There is no God." The next day the young man encountered the Rabbi and he told him he had deceived him. The Rabbi asked, "Did you go to the village as I directed?" "Yes," said the man and "I stood before the mountain and called out over and over to God, but there was no answer." The Rabbi said, "But there is no mountain there. Tell me, what did you say to God?" The young man replied, "I asked God if He was real to show Himself to me." The Rabbi said, "Well, when I go out to meet God, I confess to God my sinfulness and apart from Him I can do nothing. Then God appears to me and I gain wisdom and understanding." The next morning the young man went back to the village, fell on his knees before the mountain and said, "God, I am a sinful man, forgive me!" And when the young man looked up, the mountain had disappeared. It was only the shadow of his own self, and when self had no longer remained between him and God, it was then he saw God.

The one word that shakes the world and brings trembling to the soul is the word "God." God means more than we can comprehend and more than we can ever speak about. Awareness of God can become closer than one's own throbbing heart. The presence of God can be so overwhelming and intoxicating that it can ignite a soul on fire. When one is willing to be undone, to give up on one's public image and personal dignity, one begins to sense the presence of the Holy.

This covenant-making God initiates with His people a relationship centered in love. A longing for the heart of God and love for God permeates everything. This happens to the whole community of faith, which finds itself wanting "more of God" and God wanting all people intimately to know Him. Rabbi Schlomo Carlebach was famous for shouting to His *Hassidim*, "Don't you know you have to be drunk on God."[1] True Jews are drunk with God's love and God's love for us.

The *shekinah* (the weight of God's glory) is everywhere. No one can escape or run from God's presence. But God's manifest presence is only sensed by those who have submitted their life to Him. God's presence can be more real than the visible world around us and the next moment be as absent as if one's prayers stopped at the ceiling.

The Talmud tells the story of a Gentile who asked a Rabbi, "What purpose did your God have in speaking with Moses from the midst of a bush?" The Rabbi answered, "To teach that there is no place void of the Divine Presence, not even so lowly a thing as a bush."[2] The Jews were explicit concerning the holiness of God. God as "Father" is the distinct name of God. God's unique name *YHVH* (the tetragrammaton), revealed to the people of Israel, was always to be revered and not profaned by either their words or behavior.

The Jews were so fiercely monotheistic — there is only one true God — that even the Talmud declares, "Whoever repudiates idolatry is accounted a Jew."[3] Idolatry is the alternative vision to the Scriptural faith of God's covenantal providence. All of Scripture from Genesis to Revelation testifies to the character of God's providence and His victory over all the forces working against and trying to destroy it.[4]

This point is graphically portrayed in the Genesis account of Abraham and the sacrifice of Isaac on the Mount in Moriah. The covenant-child, Isaac, is about to be sacrificed, but the sudden appearance of a ram in the thicket provides Abraham with a burnt offering in place of his Son. So Abraham called that place, "The Lord will provide; as it is said to this day, 'On the mount of the Lord it shall be provided'" (Gen. 22:14).

There has been much questioning and attention given to God's command to Abraham to sacrifice his son, but what is not talked about much is the strong providential language of the text where the ram shows up dramatically just at the right time. This dynamic providence of God can be seen throughout all of Scripture as God continues to govern all of creation. Even what is intended as evil can be viewed through the lens of God working circumstances out for good.[5]

All of life falls under the benevolent love and rule of the Sovereign Lord God. When this radical view of life is seen through the eyes of the believer, even the smallest and seemingly most insignificant events can take on great importance. The Talmud tells the story of the difference this makes in the Hebrew mind:

> *A ship, belonging to a heathen owner, was once sailing over the sea, one of the passengers being a Jewish boy. A great storm arose, and all the Gentiles aboard took hold of their idols and prayed to them, but to no avail. Seeing that their prayers had been in vain, they said to the lad: "Call upon your God, for we have heard He answers your petitions when you cry to Him and that He is all-powerful." The boy immediately stood up and called with all his heart upon God, Who hearkened to his prayer, and the sea became calm. On reaching land, they disembarked to purchase their requirements and said to him: "Do you not wish to buy anything?" He answered: "What do you want of a poor alien like me?" They exclaimed: "You? A poor alien! We are the poor aliens; for some of us are here and have our gods in Babylon; others have them in Rome; others have their gods with them but they are no benefit to us. As for you, however, wherever you go your God is with you!"*[6]

And so the sacrament of God's *shekinah* is ever before those who have eyes of faith to see. The holy fire of God's presence continues to heal, restore, and unite people who have been separated and divided by fear and misunderstanding. The Lord God is one and is bringing Jews and Gentiles, the enslaved and the free, men and women into one new community (Gal. 5:28).

✿ | *The* Glory *of* Torah

My favorite wisdom story is about an old man and a boy who stood on a bank fishing one day:

> *They talked about many things till late in the afternoon. They talked about things such as why sunsets are red, why the rain falls, why the seasons change, and what life is like? Finally the boy looked up at the old man and asked him, "Does anybody ever see God?" The old man replied, looking over the water, "Son, it's getting so I hardly see anything else!"*

The Torah — Scripture — is a dangerous book.[1] The Torah is neither nice nor tidy, nor does it care whether or not it is "relevant." It demands surrender so it can transform us, and when we read it, in many parts of the world, it can even get us killed. We are to live life in awe and fear of the Torah, but there is also an old Rabbinic saying: "One must not be in awe of the Torah, but in awe of Him Who gives the Torah."[2] The Torah is God's Word for a return to community and to do works of love and repair the world (*tikkum olam*).

There is a Rabbinic tale of a desert country where trees and fruit were scarce and hard to come by:

> *It was said that God wanted to make sure there was enough for everyone, so He appeared to a prophet and said, "This is my commandment to the whole people for now and future generations: no one shall eat more than one fruit a day. Record this in the Holy Book. Anyone who transgresses this law will be considered to have sinned against God and against humanity. The law was faithfully observed for centuries until scientists discovered a means for turning the desert into green land. The country*

became rich in grain and livestock. And the trees bent down with the weight of unplucked fruit. But the fruit law continued to be enforced by the civil and religious authorities of the land. Anyone who pointed to the sin against humanity involved in allowing fruit to rot on the ground was dubbed a blasphemer and an enemy of morality. These people who questioned the wisdom of God's Holy Word, it was said, were not being guided by the proud spirit of faith and submission whereby alone the Truth can be received. In the churches sermons were frequently delivered in which those who broke the law were shown to have come to a bad end. Never once was mention made of the equal number of those who came to a bad end even though they faithfully kept the law, or of the vast number of those who prospered even though they broke it. Nothing could be done to change the law because the prophet who claimed to have received it from God was long since dead. He might have had the courage and the sense to change the law as circumstances changed, for he had taken God's Word, not as something to be revered, but as something to be used for the welfare of the people. As a result, some people openly scoffed at the law and at God and religion. Others broke with it secretly, and always with a sense of wrongdoing. The vast majority adhered rigorously to it and came to think of themselves as holy merely because they held on to a senseless and outdated custom they were too frightened to jettison.

The Jewish rabbis teach that the Torah is not an end in itself, but its purpose is to sanctify God's great name. The Talmud says that "when two sit and occupy themselves with the study of the Torah, the *Shekinah* is in their midst."[3] The Talmud even connects fulfilling the precepts of the Torah with receiving God's Holy Spirit.[4] The Torah leads to joyous service to God. It is like a burning song within one's heart that can never be quenched. God's Word brings divine breakthroughs, heavenly invasions of the soul, and freedom to one's spirit. It is a "living word," where word and spirit connect and incarnate themselves into one's very being. This is where the "living God" speaks and His whisper takes on human flesh.

God often comes to people in the most unexpected ways and places. Obedience to Torah means never shutting the door to the unexpected encounters of God's Word. Christians believe that God supplied the old covenant with authoritative documentation, and then the new covenant with apostolic scriptures that continue to reveal God. A God who creates a world in love and redeems the world in suffering to bring all of history and the world to completion in joyous well being.

At the beginning, the Jews as a whole did not necessarily reject Christ's followers, and Christ's followers did not reject Judaism. Jesus started a reform movement within Judaism, not a new religion. Jews and

Jewish Christians worshipped together in the synagogue and read Torah together. It was not until the destruction of the temple in 70 AD that both Judaism and Christianity started radically changing into two separate and totally distinct groups with distinct practices.[5]

The Torah describes God who gathers, scatters, and restores a messianic people. This all comes to a culmination with the triumphal coming of the Messiah which Christians see as Jesus' final return as the Messiah (which Christians understand this return as the "second coming" whereas Judaism is still waiting for the first arrival of the Messiah). The truth is both Judaism and Christianity flow out of the same stream of history and both are messianic movements.

There is much confusion and misunderstanding by both Jews and many Christians when it comes to the Jewish roots and history of their respective faiths. Jesus nowhere rejected neither His Jewishness nor Judaism. Jesus said He did not come to destroy the law but to fulfill it (Mat. 5:17–19). His debates with the Jewish religious leaders of His day were not over the authority of the Torah but over its interpretations and meaning. Jesus was completely immersed within His own history and people with no reference to some kind of history or sources outside of His own Jewish tradition.

Jesus, at times, may have seemed radical and even provocative with the many competing streams of Judaic history, but He always spoke and taught within a Jewish context and in Jewish terms. Jesus freedom to redefine issues was no greater than the freedom of earlier prophets who reworked their own living traditions, much less the freedom taken by later rabbinic teachers.

The Torah as the rule and guide to faith was so important and life-defining that Jews wore Scripture on their hands and feet when they entered to worship (Deu. 6:8–9). Scripture Torah study, meditation, and memorization of huge sections of the Tanakh was handed down from generation to generation and formed the whole basis for family life and spirituality.

Jews and Christians are people of the book and it would do neither harm to carry Scripture memory cards on their bodies, post Scripture to walls and special places of reflection in the home or work, and even commit every project or plan to a promise of God from the Scriptures. The Psalmist writes that Scripture should be the first word and last word of each day.[6]

It is God's Word that holds both Jews and Christians in a covenant relationship with Almighty God. There is a famous story of how a man came to a Rabbi for the first time in his life:

He was already advanced in years, almost forty years old. "It's the first time I have ever come to a Rabbi," the man said. The Rabbi asked him, "What did you do all your life?" The man answered, "I have gone through the Talmud four times." The Rabbi asked him, "How much of the Talmud has gone through you?"

❀ | *The* Glory *of* Shema

The master was in an expansive mood, so his disciples sought to learn from him the stages he had passed through to his quest for the divine."God first led me by the hand," he said, "into the land of action, and there I dwelt for several years. Then He returned and led me to the Land of Sorrows; there I lived until my heart was purged of every inordinate attachment. That is when I found myself in the Land of Love, whose burning flames consumed whatever was left in me of self. This brought me to the Land of Silence, where the mysteries of life and death were bared before my wondering eyes." The disciples asked the Master, "Was that the final stage of your quest?" "No," the Master said. "One day God said, 'Today I shall take you to the innermost sanctuary of the Temple, to the heart of God himself.' And I was led to the Land of Laughter."

Abraham was chosen by God to birth a new nation and teach all nations that there is but only one true God. When Abraham received the word of promise and the miracle of a son, his response was laughter. God established an everlasting covenant with Abraham and his heirs. Abraham son's name Isaac means "laughter" and Sarah said prophetically for all God's children through the ages, "God has brought me laughter, and everyone who hears about this will laugh with me." (Gen. 21:6).

The great prayer of blessing and life that springs joy and laughter is what the Jews call the *Shema*: "Hear, O Israel, the Lord our God, the Lord is One" (Deu. 6:4). The oneness of God is the foundation for both the Jewish and Christian faith. The *Shema* expresses the purpose of Israel's existence. Israel is to serve as a witness to all the nations that God is one and Lord over all the universe (see Gen. 15).

The unity of God is the basis for the unity of God's covenant people. Messianic Jews often claim that the word *echad* (one) means a compound unity whereas traditional Jews argue that it means an absolute unity. Actually, the *Shema* is not addressing either of these issues as it is that God's people are to worship God alone and no other. I can imagine an old Jewish Rabbi speaking about God and saying:

> *Consider that in our Scriptures, God was pictured as enthroned in heaven, yet at the same time he manifested himself in the cloud and the fire over the tabernacle while also putting his Spirit on his prophets. And all the while the Bible tells us that his glory was filling the universe! Do you see that God's unity is complex?*[1]

The issues of God are deep and it takes spiritual minds to discern spiritual things (1Cor. 2). I suspect Christians have read into Scripture too much in trying to prove the Trinity from the Hebrew Bible but the plurality use of words in reference to God does at least show in the Tanakh a kind of "plurality in unity" or what some refer toward the nature of God's oneness as a compound or composite unity.

The *Shema* is also at the heart of New Testament teaching. The reason why God sent His Son into the world was that through Jesus the Messiah, people in every nation and land would abandon their idols and dead religious traditions and turn to the one, true and living God. Of course, the dilemma and scandal for Jews is, how can they faithfully say the *Shema*, "Hear, O Israel, The Lord our God is one Lord" (Deu. 6:4) and also faithfully address Jesus as Thomas did, as "My Lord and my God!" (John 20:28)?

Exodus 25:8 and 2 Chronicles 6:1–2 speak about God "pitching His tent" among and with His people. God "pitched His tent" with His people Israel through the tabernacle and Temple while still remaining God in heaven and filling the whole universe with His presence. So He also pitches His tent with His Son while remaining God of heaven and continuing to fill the whole universe with His presence. The glory of God filled them both and manifested God's manifest presence. The Messiah is the visible representation of the invisible God, the living manifestation of the glory of God.

We read in Genesis 18:13–5, "Then the Lord [*YHVH*] said to Abraham. 'Why did Sarah laugh, saying, "Shall I in truth bear a child, old as I am?" Is anything too wondrous for the Lord [*YHVH*]? I will return to you at this time next year, and Sarah shall have a son.'"

Sarah lied, saying, "I did not laugh," for she was frightened.

But He replied, "You did laugh."

The natural reading of the text is one of the three men was none other than "The Lord" Himself. It is incredible to not only read that the

Lord God talked to Abraham and Sarah as a man, but He even sat down and ate their food! The whole story of Scripture is God wants to get closer and closer to His people.

God is calling all nations and all people, both Jews and Gentiles together as one holy family. The darkness of the world filled with pride, stubbornness, unbelief, and disunity veils a sleeping world from seeing the dawn of a new horizon, the glorious son of a new day, the unending light of a glorious tomorrow. God is calling Jews and Christians to unite so that the whole world can see their destinies crisscross and the whole world witness the brilliant glory of a visible, united people of God.

There is a tale of a Rabbi who sat near a campfire with a group of students. He asked the question, "How can we know when the night has ended and the day has begun?" Looking up at the stars, one of the students offered an answer. "You know the night is over and the day has begun when you can look into the distance and deduce which animal is your dog and which is your sheep." The Rabbi replied, "This is a good answer, but it is not the answer I am looking for." Another student spoke. "You know the night is over and the day has begun when the sunlight falls upon the leaves and you can tell the difference between a palm tree and a fig tree." "Again a good answer," the Rabbi said. "But it is not the answer I am looking for." Unable to think of other answers to the riddle, the students finally said, "Tell us, Rabbi. Answer your own question. How can one tell when the night is over and the day has begun?" The Rabbi answered, "When you can look into the eyes of a human being and see a friend, you know that it is morning. If you cannot see a friend, you know it is still night."

❀ | *The* Glory *of* Covenant

Rabbi Simcha Bunem said to Rabbi Chanoch, "Cite some verse of the Torah, and I will reveal its meaning to you." Rabbi Chanoch immediately said, "And Moses spoke in the ears of the people of all the people of Israel the words of the poem, until their completion." Rabbi Scimcha Bunem shouted, "until their completion... until their completion." Rabbi Chanoch said, "But all you did was repeat the final words of the text twice." Chanoch complained, "This is nothing. What did you hear in this that brings you such joy?" Rabbi Simcha Bunem chided his friend and said, "You are not a fool! Figure it out!" "All right," Rabbi Chanoch frowned, "Lets see... 'And Moses spoke in the ears of all the people of Israel the words of this poem, until their completion.' If Moses had been referring to the completion of the poem, he would have said, 'until its completion.' Because he spoke in the plural, he wasn't referring to the poem at all but to the people themselves. So he said, 'until their completion!' Until their perfection! So the words of the poem remind us that our covenant with God will be repeated and repeated in each of our ears until it transforms each of our hearts. "We are never abandoned; God never despairs of us and will teach us continually until we perfectly live the godliness we are called to embody!" "That's it!" cried Rabbi Simcha Bunem, and the two men danced with joy.

God's electing love is what stands behind His covenant with Israel. The concept of covenant (*berith*) is conditional based in many clauses like "If you follow my laws..." Covenant is a partnership between two parties and therefore shows mutuality between God and Israel. God initiates the covenant and Israel responds to live in accordance with God's ways.

It is interesting to note the Rabbis emphasized the divine freedom of God and the human side of man's freedom to choose to follow God's covenant laws.[1] The backdrop to all this is love language which shows the love relationship between God and Israel which can only be entered into freely to be genuine love. Love can not be coerced or forced. Throughout the Hebrew Bible, God's vulnerable love is displayed where God actually "risks" to love a particular people.[2] Israel is free to accept the covenant or reject it. This covenant relationship extends over every part of life:

> God's covenant is "concerned with rulers and enemies, pots and pans, genitals and offspring. The covenant matters because it lays claim to matter and refuses to be relegated to the nonmaterial realm. It is not up in the heavens or out across the sea where it cannot be found much less practiced, but it is 'very close to you, in your mouth and in your heart, to observe it' (Deu. 30:14). Israel's covenant with God lies close to home, close to the mouth and heart, close to everyday things."[3]

One can also see Torah is at the heart of covenant because it sets the stage for how Israel is set apart for a life of holiness. God is forming a Torah shaped people who live Torah shaped lives. This is a life of holiness, joy, passionate love and peace. The whole covenant looks forward toward Israel's deliverance from exile where the coming Messiah would usher in a Kingdom of peace. God's covenant of peace moves from the chosen ones out to the whole world. God's covenant with Israel extends towards God's coming reign of peace for all of humanity.

Whatever Jeremiah's "new covenant" looks like, it will still be a covenant with Israel. Romans 11 says that the Gentiles are grafted into the branch of Israel and are not supposed to be some separate distinct group from Israel. Covenant therefore is a form of communal relationship established by God and appropriated by faith and commitment. God blessing the children of Abraham also is to be a blessing to all the nations. God stands with a particular people in the world but He also stands with and for the world (nations).

There is such a mutual give and take between Israel and God that even Rabbinic reflection captures the deep love between each of them. The Israelites say:

> Hear O Israel, the Lord thy God, the Lord is One (ehad). And the Holy Spirit calls the heavens and says, "Who is like unto thee, O Israel, a people unique (ehad) upon the earth." The Israelites say, "Who is like unto thee, O Lord, among the gods?" And the Holy Spirit calls from heaven and says, "Happy art thou, O Israel, who is like thee?" The Israelites reply, "Who is like the Lord, who answers us whenever we call upon him?;" and the Holy Spirit cries out and says, "What nation has God

near it like Israel?" The Israelites say, "Thou art the glory of their strength;" and the Holy Spirit cries out, "Israel, in thee I will be glorified."[4]

Israel is unique and chosen by God because God loves her and is one (*ehad*). Covenant names both the ground rules and the playing field where all her activities and life choices are carried out. The covenant defines the boundaries for God's people as well as God's Lordship or Kingship over all creation. There is nothing that does not come under the rule and power of God Almighty.

One of the earliest prayers in Hebrew liturgy starts with the words:

"With great love hast Thou loved us, O Lord our God, with great and exceeding pity hast Thou pitied us. Our Father, our King, for our father's sake, who trusted in Thee, and whom Thou didst teach the statues of life, be also gracious unto us and teach us." The Rabbis would also pray, "Our Father, our King, we have sinned before Thee. Our Father, our King, we have no king beside Thee. Our Father, our King, have compassion upon us."[5]

The covenant that God established with Israel is for the redemption and restoration of all of creation. God's leadership covers everything. The covenant draws a sinful humanity close to the heart of God which is full of compassion and grace. God's covenant capture people's hearts by the very heart of God. God's covenant is to extend the rule of God over all creation, even calling those parts back which are in rebellion to the ways of God. God the King, through covenant, is restoring all kingdoms under the realm of the one true and rightful King and eternal Kingdom. It is here that eternity crosses from the twilight into the dawn of destiny where the long awaited Messiah finally heals the whole world.

❊ *The* Glory *of* Election

The people of Israel were not the first to whom God offered His Torah. Indeed, before He approached the children of Isaac and Jacob, He offered His precious teaching to the children of Ishmael and Esau. When the Lord God summoned the children of Ishmael, he asked them, "Do you desire my Torah?" "What is written in it?" they wanted to know. God answered, "Thou shall not kill." "Heaven forbid!" they said. "We don't want it! This Torah is Yours and Yours it shall remain. We want no part of it." One of them by the name Samael spoke up and said, "But if you are seeking a people for whom such a law is fitting, look to the sons of Jacob." Samael suggested the Israelites to God in the conviction that they would fail to live the Torah and would then by wiped off the face of the earth for the transgression. Then God went to the children of Esau. God asked them, "Do you desire My Torah?" "What is written in it?" they wanted to know. "Thou shall not commit adultery," God answered. They responded, "Alas, we cannot accept it. Offer your Torah to the children of Isaac. They are more suited for it than we." "But you are the firstborn," God protested, "Its yours by your birthright." "Then let our birthright be given to the children of Isaac." Then God summoned the prophets and holy ones who had been appointed to lead the other nations of the world. To them too, He offered His Torah, but they too, refused. In His divine heart of hearts God rejoiced that He might give His Torah to the Israelites, like a physician with a phial filled with exiler of life, who longs to keep it for his beloved son. Said the physician to himself, "If the servants in my house knew that I intended to give this precious gift to my own son, they would grow jealous of him and seek to kill him." What did the physician do? He took a touch a poison and smeared it around the end of the phial. Next he summoned his servants and said, "Since you are my faithful servants, I offer you this life-giving drug. Would you care to try it?" "First let us see what it is," they replied. No sooner did they take a taste of the drug than they fell ill. "If the doctor gives this drug to his son," they thought to themselves, "the child will surely die, and we shall inherit the master's wealth." "Master, this wondrous medicine is fit only for your son," they declared to the physician. "We do not deserve such a fine reward for our humble labor. Give it to your beloved child."Like the wise physician, God knew if He gave the Torah to Israel without first offering it to the other nations of the world, they would pursue His chosen and seek to kill them for the Torah they had received. In this way the people of Israel inherited God's most precious possession, His Torah, which they shared with the world.

This precious gift, according to the Talmud that Israel received was the medium of suffering, the Torah, the land, and the World to Come.[1] Israel is God's chosen people not because of favoritism from God but because as God's firstborn son, they bear a heavier responsibility. The rewards are great as well as the liabilities and punishment. The Talmud says that "because God loved Israel He multiplied their sufferings."[2] God is a holy God who is always making His people holy. Israel's purpose and election and duty is to imitate the King.

Election is based in God's covenant relationship with Israel. God's chosen people are the historically elected descendants of Abraham and Sarah whose life and choices are shaped by Torah and their covenant with God. Israel is both called into a life with God through the Torah and called out from among the nations to be a peculiar people set apart for God. But it would be a mistake for people to understand this election as some kind of private or individualistic thing. Israel's election is communal. "God does not choose individuals and then make them part of community, but rather God chooses a people, a family, and within that family lays claim to all who are a part of it."[3]

Although God's election meant that God sided with Israel (Deu. 4:37–38), He refused to ignore her disobedience (Deu. 4:39–40). Israel is continually reminded by the prophets that her election is a responsibility toward righteous conduct for God and her neighbors. God desires His will to be obeyed and Israel is to display virtues like humility, obedience, justice, and compassion. God's election of Israel gave no blanket approval of all she did nor could it even guarantee political success.

Israel's election owes it existence not to anything concerning herself but on the unmerited grace and faithfulness of God. Israel's election is both eternal and unconditional in the sense that election is not based upon Israel's faith or faithfulness but on the faithfulness of the One who chooses. "The unconditionality of election simply reflects the conviction that election is God's work."[4] Unlike modern man's concern that focuses on rational individualistic choice, the Jewish biblical understanding of election is rooted unapologetically in God's prior choice.

Despite Israel's disobedience, God will not cast the Jews away, for God's election is trustworthy. It is precisely through the people of Israel that God has promised to bless and redeem all the nations. God's redemption begins with God's chosen people and then reaches out toward all the world. Even though many Jews have rejected Yeshua the Messiah, the final restoration of Israel in the end leads to the final redemption of humanity. Just as God called Abraham and promised him, "I will make of you a great nation... and in you all the families of the earth shall be blessed" (Gen. 12:3). Rather than Israel becoming one nation dominating and coercing all other nations, scripture depicts her as a nation that brings blessing and peace to all other nations.

One can also see in scripture how not only blessing but even punishment is a corporate and communal affair for Israel. For example, Achan's family is punished for Achan's disobedience and sin (Jos. 7) as well as Korah's rebellion (Num. 16). Although election happens individually to prophets, priests, and kings, there is a strong corporate aspect of election throughout the whole of scripture. Israel is portrayed in the Hebrew Bible as the "people" of God, the collective "Bride" of Yahweh. Corporately then, Israel is a treasured possession of God. God's election of Israel is a call to serve the world. The whole world waits and groans for the Messiah to come and claim His Bride.

✳ *The* Glory *of* Israel

Rabbi Abraham had lived an exemplary life. And when his time arrived, he left this world surrounded by the blessing of his congregation, who come to regard him as a saint and as the principal cause of all the blessings they had received from God. It was no different at the other end, for the angels came forward to welcome him with shouts of praise. Throughout the festivities the Rabbi seemed withdrawn and distressed. He kept his head in his hands and refused to be comforted. He was finally taken before the Judgment Seat where he felt himself enveloped by a Loving Kindness that was infinite. He heard a Voice of infinite tenderness say to him, "What is it that distresses you, my son?" "Most Holy One," replied the Rabbi, "I am unworthy of all the honors that are bestowed on me here. Even though I was considered to be an example to 'the people, there must have been something wrong with my life, for my only son, in spite of my example and my teaching, abandoned our faith and became a Christian." "Let that not disturb you, my son. I understand exactly how you feel, for I have a son who did the same thing!"

The whole Jewish-Christian schism has been an unfortunate episode of human history. First, some of the Jewish religious leaders rejected the teachings and mission of the early church and then later, the church rejected many Jews and their religious heritage. How is it that reform can lead so easily into the sin of schism?[1] How can the roots say to the branches I have no need of you or vise versa? Despite the sad history between the synagogue and church, Jesus is still the Messiah for both Jews and Gentiles. We live in a new day where more Jews and Christians than ever are coming together in a spirit of love, blessing, and community. The birth pangs of the end are beginning and the church is experiencing what Hosea predicted: Israel coming "trembling to the

Lord" (Hos. 3:5).

The whole redemption of the world is drawing near as Luke 21:28 prophetically points to. Gentiles are repenting for centuries long anti-Semitism and once again discovering the Jewish roots of the early church. A love for the Jewish people is sovereignly being poured out into the hearts of the Gentile Church. "Israel" literally means "one who struggles with God." God is calling Jews and Gentiles to struggle together in their faith for Him. Christians are suddenly awakening to Scriptures like Ezekiel 37 which is not a vision describing a dead church that needs revival but a glorious vision of the restoration of Israel. The text specifically says, "These bones are the whole house Israel. I will settle (them) in (their) own land" (Eze. 37:11,14). We are living in the fulfillment of Zachariah's prophecy, "Ten men from all languages and nations will take hold of one Jew by the hem of the robe" and say "let us go with you, because we have heard that God is with you" (Zec. 8:23).

Just as Jesus' parable of the prodigal son has many implications with the restoration of the nation of Israel, even the Talmud tells it own story of Israel leaving and returning and final restoration.[2] This parable goes like this:

> *A king's son fell into evil ways. The king sent his tutor to him with the message, "Return, O my son." But the son sent to his father the reply, "With what can I return? I am ashamed to come before you." Then the father sent to him, saying: "Can a son be ashamed to return to his father? If you return, do not return to your father?"*[3]

God always rejoices when one of His children comes home. He is the loving Father who blesses with out stretched arms and may even scandalously be the one running ahead to meet wayward sons and daughters.[4]

The Jews are God's stake in human history. No wonder the Devil has tried to destroy them so many times to undermine the eternal plans of God. Christians need to face the difficult question, "Is it really God's will that there be no Judaism in the world?" Would it really be the triumph of God if the Torah scrolls were no longer read in the synagogues, that no more ancient prayers be said in Hebrew which Jesus Himself prayed, and what would the world be like without the witness and example of the Jews? Israel is here to stay because God wishes it.[5]

The Talmud says that the Messiah would bring about the reunion of all the tribes of Israel.[6] Not only is there an unprecedented return to Israel by Jews around the world but countries from all over the world are sending back missionaries as their thank offering to the Holy Land.[7] God is shaking the world with Israel at the epicenter. God is re-gathering Israel to reveal His own love and destiny for the world. As the growth of the church exponentially explodes in the southern hemisphere of the world, this "global Christian" move of God is leading the way to what some call the "back to Jerusalem" movement.

This is not some evangelize Jerusalem campaign but it is a sharing of the Messiah for all unreached people groups from the East all the way back to the Middle East. Jerusalem was the starting point of the gospel two thousand years ago and it has now circled the whole globe and is returning to its starting point. There are so many divine "reversals" in the teachings of Yeshua/Jesus, and this last outpouring of God's Spirit upon Israel and all nations may fulfill His own prophetic words, "Thus the last shall be first and the first last" (Mat. 20:16).

Jews and Christians have to each find their own way back to their common roots and Messianic origins. The church and Israel have clashed with each other but a new day is dawning where they will no longer collide with each other but love and serve one another. When push comes to shove, the world may even see them lay their lives down and die for each other

One of the oldest churches is the Ethiopian Church which has long held to its Jewish origins and historic liturgy which still has a strong Jewish flavor. This ancient Jewish-Christian tradition from the Eastern Orthodox in Africa tells a wonderful story from "The Wisdom of the Elders of Ethiopia":

> About discretion and patience... They told how some men, having heard of Abbu Agaton's reputation, came to him with the intention of testing his discretion and patience, to see if he could be made angry. They said to him, "Are you Agaton? We have heard what a great fornicator you are!" He gave thanks and said to them, "That is correct, that's just what I am!" Again they said, "Are you the Agaton who is such a slanderer and calumniator of men?" "'Yes," he said, "that's who I am." Then they said to him, "Are you not Agaton the heretic?" At this he answered and said, "No, I am not! A heretic I have never been!" And he was angry! So they inquired further and said to him, "Tell us why you willingly bore what we said at first, but our last remark you will not tolerate at all?" He replied, "I took what you said first, because it was good for me to do so; but were I to declare myself a heretic, I would be separating myself from the Lord!" Hearing this statement, they marveled at him and went away edified.[8]

❀ The Glory of Authority

Once the conqueror Alexander entered the Land of Israel, he decided to test the sages to see whether they were, indeed, as wise as they were said to be. "I want you all to answer me truthfully." Alexander began, "And have no fear for your lives. Tell me, please, who is called wise?" "He who can see what will come to pass," they told him. "For the wise know where they are and where they have been according to where they are going." "Then who is called mighty?" Alexander continued. "He is mighty," they answered, "who can subdue his evil inclination. For a man cannot rule a world if he cannot rule himself." "Who, then, is a rich man?" the conqueror asked. "One who rejoices in what God has given him," they replied. "For it is better to want what you have than to have what you want. And he who wants more is forever in want." Impressed by their reply, Alexander put to them yet another question: "What must a man do in order to have life?" "He must offer up his life," they declared to him, "to the study of Torah, prayer, and acts of loving kindness. For to have life is to impart life to others." "And if a man wants to kill himself?" Alexander pressed the matter. "What then should he do?" "If he would kill himself," they answered, "then he should try to engage in every selfish or selfish indulgence. For to consume life is to be consumed." "How should a man go about making himself popular?" "He should renounce all sovereignty and authority over others," the sages told Alexander. "For he is loved who is a servant to his fellow human being." Now this reply disturbed Alexander, who was known for his authority over all the world. Therefore, thinking to divide the sages against one another, he asked, "Which among you is the wisest?" "We are all equally wise," they answered him, "since we have all agreed on the answers we have given you." Realizing that he could not trick them, the mighty conqueror finally asked, "Why do you resist me?" "We do not resist you," they explained, "but Satan who is acting through you. For he has been given power, so that you might test us." "Are you not afraid that I will have you all killed?" Alexander pretended to threaten them. "You will do us no harm," they replied, "for in bringing us here together, you have promised us safe conduct, and it would be unfitting for a king to go back on his word. "Very much pleased with these last words, Alexander dressed the sages in purple, placed gold chains on their necks, and sent them on their way. He was convinced of the wisdom and the holiness of the people of Israel.

All authority under heaven and earth is given by God and no one has any authority that God has not granted someone. God's authority in the Hebrew Bible is unalterable and is universal over all other powers and authorities (Exo. 15:6–11; Psa. 29:10; Dan. 4:34–35). God's power and might is over all kingdoms and nations and God can do whatever He pleases (Jer.18:6; also see Rom.9:21).

All people are called under the subjection of God's authority, and all people are to live for His glory. One sees throughout the Hebrew Bible that God exercised authority through prophets, priests, and kings who were to proclaim His message (Jer. 1:7ff), teach God's laws (Deu 31:11; Mal. 2:7) and rule in accordance to those laws (Deu. 17:18–20).

All power and authority among human rulers and powers is delegated from God. The whole Jewish way of life is to respect the authority and rules God has given for family and community. The Talmud goes into great detail dealing with the authority and laws of the state and civil laws of the land that the people are to submit to and follow.[1] Even the Torah is referred to as "the power of God." All faithful followers of God are under the authority of the Word of God which comes from God.

The Messiah is one who comes in the power and authority of God. Jesus came in the power of God's Spirit (Luke 4:14–18) and His whole identity, mission, and authority derived from His Father in heaven (see John 5:19). His authority over demons, death, sin, sickness, and nature (Mark 1:22; Mat. 9:6: Luke 8:4) was a result of His obedience to the Father. Jesus' life, death, and resurrection disarmed the principalities and powers (John 12:31) which He received all authority from His heavenly Father over heaven and earth (Mat. 28:18; Col. 1:16–20).

People were amazed that Jesus not only taught "as one with authority" but they marveled at His mighty works and were astonished at His wisdom (Mark 1:27; Luke 4:36; Mat. 13:54; Mark 6:2). The picture of Jesus we find in the four gospels is that important people kneel at Jesus feet (Mark 5:22; 10:17); disciples follow him without question (Mark 1:17 –20; 2:14); and even the demons recognize Jesus' power and authority (Mark 1:24; 3:11; 5:7; 9:20).

Even outsiders like a Roman Centurion guard recognized the authority and power of Jesus (Luke 7:8 "I, too, am a man under authority…"). The religious authorities questioned Jesus about His power and authority (Mark 11:28). The aim of their questions was to expose Jesus' lack of authority. The very questions they asked Jesus demonstrates a recognition by Jesus opponents that His words and actions embodied a claim to high authority.

As Jesus announced the arrival of God's Kingdom and did the work of the Messiah, He says in Mark 2:10, "so that you might know the son of man has the authority on earth to forgive sins…" Even when John the Baptist began to have doubts and sent His disciples to question Jesus, Jesus replied to them, "Go back and report to John what you hear and see: the blind receive sight, the lame walk, those have leprosy are cured, the deaf hear, the dead are raised, and the good news is preached to the poor. Blessed is the man who does not fall away on account of me" (Mat. 11:4–6).

In Yeshua/Jesus, the Messiah, the Kingdom of God had arrived in power and glory (Mat. 12:28; Luke 11:20). Jesus did not live for Himself but for the Kingdom of God and for others. So also are the Messiah's followers to live. His disciples are to go in His name and with His authority (Mark 16:15–21; John 20:21). As the gathered people of God go in Jesus' name, they will even do greater things as Jesus' presence goes with them in power to and among all the nations (John 14:12–14).

The Glory of Blessing

When he was advanced in years, Rabbi Yochanan ben Zakkai fell mortally ill. Hearing of this, his disciples decided to visit their ailing teacher. They arrived at the rabbi's home and were shown to the room where he lay dying. When they went in to see him, the sick man took one look at them and began to weep. Surprised at their teacher's tears and hardly able to withhold their own, the disciples said, "O lamp of Israel, pillar of God's right hand, mighty hammer! Tell us, please, why you weep?"He replied, "If I were being taken this day before a human king — who breathes now but tomorrow who will lie in the grave, whose anger with me would not last forever, who may imprison me for a time but not for all eternity, who indeed may send me to my death but not to death everlasting, and whom I might persuade with words or bribe with money — even then I might be brought to tears. "But, you see, the One I go to is the Almighty King of kings, the Holy One, blessed be He, without whom there is no life and whose life endures for all eternity. The anger He may direct at me is an everlasting anger, and if He imprisons me, it is an eternal imprisonment. If he puts me to death, it is a death without end, and there is no persuading Him with words or bribing Him with money. Don't you understand? When two paths stretch out before me, one leading to Paradise, the other to Hell, and I do not know which is mine, do I not have cause to weep? Surely you can see that? Have I taught you nothing?" The rabbi, his eyes red from weeping, fell silent and stared at his disciples. Would they indeed understand the tears he had shed? Finally they broke the silence and said to him, "Master, bless us." At that moment the rabbi saw the opportunity to convey to them what troubled him. And so, without hesitation, he conferred upon them this blessing: "May it be God's will that the fear of heaven will be upon you as much as our fear of flesh and blood." Having expected something more elaborate and much more profound, the disciples looked at one another, rather puzzled, and said, "Is that all?" Their teacher answered

them, "You think it such an easy and simple matter? Oh, if you only could at-
tain so much! When a man acts not according to the will of God but according
to his own will and commits transgression, what does he say to himself? He
says, 'I hope no one will see me. I hope no one will find out.' But know that there
is One who always sees, whose eyes never close. He knows the innermost secrets
of your heart, and he always finds out. When you stand before Him, He will ask
you about what He already knows — and what you have yet to confess, perhaps
even to yourself. Let His question be my last blessing."

Jewish blessings of praise describe the character and qualities of God.
Blessings sensitize us to the presence of God in and through the world
around us. The words "know before whom you stand" is a custom for
those in the synagogue to know and understand to whom their petitions
and words were being addressed to. A common Jewish blessing and
prayer is as follows:

> *Blessed are You, O Lord our God and God of our fathers,*
> *God of Abraham, God of Isaac, and God of Jacob.*
> *The great, mighty, and awesome God;*
> *Supreme God,*
> *Who performs acts of lovingkindness,*
> *Creator of all,*
> *Remembering the faithfulness of the fathers*
> *And lovingly bringing the redeemer to their descendants*
> *For His own sake.*
> *Helping, saving, and protecting king!*
> *Blessed are You, O Lord, protector of Abraham.*[1]

God is a personal God who is spoken about in personal terms. He directs
the affairs of man and brings redemption to Israel through the covenant.
We do not seek a blessing from God alone but we stand in a great tradition of people as descendants of God's covenant people.

Among the Jewish blessings is the expectation of the miracle of
resurrection:[2]

> *You are mighty forever, O Lord.*
> *Reviver of the dead are You,*
> *Powerful to save.*
> *Causing the wind to blow and the rain to fall.*
> *Sustaining the living with steadfast kindness.*
> *Reviving the dead with great mercy.*
> *Upholding the fallen,*

Healing the sick,
Freeing the fettered,
And keeping faith with those who sleep in the dust.
Who is like You, master of might.
who is similar to You,
King who brings death and revives and causes salvation
        to spring forth.
Faithful are You to revive the dead.
Blessed are You, O Lord, reviver of the dead.[3]

In Hebrew thought, Jewish blessings were not just descriptions of God but were qualities to be imitated.[4] God's people are to imitate God through loving deeds like helping the poor, visiting the sick and those in prison, and feeding the hungry.[5] Praise and gratitude are one's response to God's blessing in serving others.

The Jewish blessings show the belief of God's goodness over all creation. Blessing God is a full recognition of His Lordship and sovereignty. There is a mistaken notion among Christians to bless the food at mealtimes.[6] One does not bless the object but rather God who is the giver of all good things.[7]

There is the standard liturgical formulation pronouncing a blessing from the book of Numbers: "The Lord bless you and keep you! The Lord make His Face to shine upon you and be gracious unto you! The Lord lift up His countenance to you and grant you peace" (6:24 26). Built on a pattern of three increasing steps — three Hebrew words in the first blessing, five in the second, and the sacred number seven in the third — this blessing finally concludes with the promise of shalom, peace. God's peace of "wholeness" and "completeness" is a blessing of the end for the present and for inward peace to break forth in outward world peace. So, we pray for the greatest blessing of all, the Messiah to come and bring shalom to all of creation: "*Maranatha*… Amen!"

✺ | *The* Glory *of* Grace

One day Rabbi Baruch was busy studying the Torah, when his little grandson Yechiel came running to him. The Rabbi could see that the child was very upset and immediately asked him, "What is the matter my young one?" In tears, the little boy cried, "Grandfather, Grandfather, it isn't fair!" "Tell your grandfather all about it," the Rabbi replied. "What isn't fair?" "I was playing hide-and-seek with my friend," Yechiel explained through his sobs. "He hid first, and I looked for him until I found him. Then it was my turn. I hid in a good hiding place, Grandfather, and he started to look for me. But when he couldn't find me right away, he just gave up. He stopped looking for me and left me there all by myself! It just isn't fair!" Rabbi Baruch gave his grandson a loving caress, and, with tears welling up in his own eyes, said, "There, now, Yechiel, I'll tell you a secret. You are not the only one who is sad because no one is looking for him. God is unhappy too, for the same reason that you are unhappy. You see, like you, He is in hiding, and no one is looking for him. People look for and long for all sorts of things, for everything except God. Do you realize what that means, little one? Because we do not try to find Him, we ourselves are lost!"

The grace of God is a central tenet of the whole Bible and yet many people seem to miss this golden thread that is intertwined throughout all of holy Scripture.[1] Jewish teaching rightly balances God's grace with divine justice. The Talmud says, "When the Holy One, blessed be He, came to create the first man He foresaw both righteous and wicked would issue from him. He said, 'If I create him, wicked men will issue from him?' What did He do? He removed the wicked from before Him, allied the attribute of mercy with Himself and created him."[2]

The Talmud likens justice and mercy with cold and hot water which flow together. The Talmud says, "If I create the world only with the attribute of mercy, sins will multiply beyond all bounds. If I create only with the attribute of justice, how can the world last? Behold, I will create it with both attributes; would that it might endure!."[3]

The Rabbis delighted in calling God Rachmana (the merciful) and taught that "the world is judged by grace."[4] Victory of good over evil comes from God's righteous mercy. God is seen as one who is slow to anger and shows long-suffering for the wicked. "Even in the time of His anger He remembers mercy."[5]

God is slow to wrath and displays great compassion and mercy. God's mercy subdues His wrath and His throne is a throne of mercy.[6] As man is made in the divine image, so is man to show mercy toward those around him. One of the crowning virtues of man is showing mercy to others.

The Talmud lists seven crowing virtues of man, and mercy is one of them. They are faith, righteousness, justice, lovingkindness, mercy, truth, and peace.[7] The whole relationship between man and God rests on these virtues, which God's Spirit produces within His creatures.

The starting, the middle, and the end of life with God is a life full of God's grace. Grace makes all the difference because no amount of good works can attain what God does through His grace in humble vessels of clay. Second Corinthians 2:7–10 says:

> But we have this treasure in earthen vessels, that the excellence of the power may be of God and not of us. We are hard-pressed on every side, yet not crushed; we are perplexed, but not in despair; persecuted, but not forsaken; struck down, but not destroyed — always carrying about in the body the Messiah, that his life may also be manifested in our body.

And so, "For by grace [in and through the Messiah] you have been saved through faith, and not of yourselves; it is the gift of God, not of works, lest anyone should boast" (Eph. 2:8–9). God has destined us a vessels for His glory that through good works, the Messiah's love and light may shine through us for all creation to see.

> Long ago, whenever the world was in need of rain, the sages would send word to Abba Chilkiah, grandson of Choni the Circle Drawer, asking that he pray for rain. Like his grandfather before him, Abba Chilkiah would honor their request, and his prayers would be granted. On one occasion, when the land was especially parched from drought, the rabbi sent two scholars to personally seek out Abba Chilkiah and plead with him to pray for rain. They came to his house and asked for him, but he was not there. Recalling that Abba Chilkiah worked for his bread, they went to the fields

outside of the town to look for him. Sure enough, they found him hard at work with a hoe. Pleased to have come to him at last, the scholar extended a greeting to Abba Chilkiah. But he said nothing in reply. The scholars were puzzled by his failure to answer, but they waited patiently and respectfully for Abba Chilkiah to acknowledge them. And as they waited, he worked. Before long evening approached, and Abba Chilkiah gathered up some wood and his hoe. The wood and the hoe he placed on one shoulder, and over the other he threw his cloak. Then he set out for his home with the two scholars following behind him. Upon reaching his home, his wife greeted him and let the two strangers in the house. They sat down and ate a meal together. When the meal was finished, he said to his wife, "I know that these scholars have come to ask me to pray for rain. Come with me, then, to the roof, and we shall offer our supplication to God. Perhaps the Holy One, blessed be He, will have mercy and the rain will come, without any credit due to us." The two scholars followed Abba Chilkiah to the roof, where he took up a position in one corner, while his wife stood in another. As soon as the prayer came to his lips, clouds began to form over the place where his wife stood, and it began to rain. When they all had returned inside, Abba Chilkiah finally spoke to the two scholars. "Why have you come here?" he asked them, just to be sure that he had guessed rightly. "We came to implore you to pray for rain," they replied. At that Abba Chilkiah exclaimed, "Blessed be God, who has deemed that you are no longer dependent on Abba Chilkiah! For this rain had come not due to my merit but by the mercy of God." "We believe, sir," they said, "that the rain has indeed come on your account. But we do not understand the meaning of the mysterious way you have acted. Why, for example, did you ignore us when we greeted you?" "I hired out my labor to work the whole day," he explained, "and I said that I would not relax on the job." And the clouds?" they inquired. "Why did they first appear where your wife stood, and only afterward over the corner where you were? Said Abba Chilkiah, "Because my wife stays at home and offers bread to the poor, which they can enjoy at once. I merely give them money, which they cannot enjoy at once. Therefore she is closer to God than I am." Then after a moment of further reflection, he remarked, "Or perhaps it may have to do with certain thieves in our neighborhood. I prayed that they might die, but she prayed that they might repent. And they repented, for her prayers were more righteous than mine." Hearing this, the two scholars were amazed and rejoiced at what they had seen and witnessed.

✾ | *The* Glory *of the* Law

After he had delivered the Israelites from the bondage of Egypt with the help of God, Moses led them to Mount Sinai. There Moses ascended the heights to receive from God the revelation that he was to offer to all of Israel. When God had finished speaking the words He wanted to speak, Moses descended from the mountain, bearing the Torah and the Law which the Holy One, blessed be He, had entrusted to him, eager to offer the great treasure to the people of Israel. All the while, however, Satan had stood by, awaiting the opportunity to lay claim of the Torah and the Law to make it his own. When he saw Moses leave the presence of the Lord, he approached the Holy One and said, "Sovereign of the Universe, please tell me, where is the Torah and the Law?" "I have given it to the earth," the Lord answered him. Satan descended to the earth, approached it and asked, "Where is the Torah and the Law?" But the earth replied, "God alone traces the path of the wisdom you seek, for He sees all things, even unto the ends of the earth. Go, then, and look to the ends of the earth." After Satan looked and could not find it, he returned to God and asked, "Sovereign of the Universe! I have searched the world over and cannot find the Torah and the Law anywhere." "Go, then," God answered him, "and seek out the son of Amram." Hearing these words, Satan hastened off to Moses and said, "Tell me, son of Amram, where is the Torah and the Law that the Holy One, blessed be He, entrusted to you?" But Moses replied, "Who am I, that the Lord God should give me something so precious as His Torah and Law?" Hearing Moses reply, God reproached him, saying, "Moses, would you be a liar?" "Sovereign of the Universe!" said Moses. "You entrusted the treasure of Your Torah and Your Law to me. Should I be so bold as to keep it only for myself? Surely it was not intended for me alone but for all the children of Israel." The Holy One, blessed be He, replied, "Moses, because you have humbled yourself and have set above yourself the Torah and My Law and gave it to the children of Israel for whom it was in-

tended, My teaching will be called by your name." So it is written in the words of the prophet Malachi, "Remember the Torah and the Law of My servant Moses."

God gave the Torah and His Law to Moses which is called *YHVH*'s Torah (1Ch. 16:40; Neh. 9:3; and Jos. 24:26, for example) and Moses' Torah (2Ch. 23:18; 35:12; Jos. 8:31; 23:6 and elsewhere). The Law covered every area of social and religious life of Israel. Everything Israel did was to be established by God's Word and His covenant relationship with His people.[1]

The Jewish way of life is not about following some legalistic code or rules but is governed by the grace and mercy of a Loving God.[2] Rabbi Shammai notes that Moses gave 365 prohibitions and 248 positive commands in the Law. David in Psalm 15 reduces them to eleven; Isaiah 33:14–15 made them six; Micah 6:8 binds them into three; and Habakkuk 2:4 reduces them all to one, namely, "The just shall live by faith."[3]

Matthew 23:3 says, "The Scribes and the Pharisees sit at Moses seat." Jewish authority was established on the authority of Moses. Even the Apostle Paul who is often misunderstood on his teachings of the Law did not abolish the Law but saw its fulfillment in Christ.[4] One can see throughout the Newer Testament teachings a confirmation of the Jewish moral tradition rooted ultimately in Torah.[5] All of the law is fulfilled in the Messiah. As people are led by the Spirit of God, they fulfill "the law of the Messiah" (see Gal. 5:18 and 6:2).

The Roman emperor Hadrian issued a decree in the Land of Israel prohibiting the study, teaching, and practice of the Torah on pain of torture and death. But there was one who feared God more than he feared men. Rabbi Akiva, who persisted in publicly expounding the Torah and openly defying the Roman Order. So the Romans arrested him and cast him into prison to wait his terrible fate:

Rabbi Akiva's friend Pappus Ben Yehudah was also arrested and was imprisoned in the cell next to him. Upon discovering the rabbi in the adjoining cell, Pappus cried out, "Happy are you, Rabbi Akiva! For you have at least been arrested for your devotion to the Torah. But woe to Pappus! I have been imprisoned as a result of my involvement in idle and meaningless affairs." Before long the Roman guards came for Rabbi Akiva. It was the hour designated for the recitation of the Shema. Rabbi Akiva could not let the hour pass without saying his prayers. As the torturers mutilated his aged flesh with iron rakes, he raised his cry to the heaven and began shouting, "Shema Yisrael! Hear, O Israel!" Now thanks either to the cruelty of the Romans or to their mercy — who can say which? — the rabbi's disciples were allowed to come and be with him in his last hour. But when they heard their teacher cry out the prayer in the midst of being tortured, they pleaded with him saying, "Master, even to this point? Will you sing your praises to God even as you endure this terrible torture?" "All of my life I have been haunted by the commandment that you are to love the Lord God 'with all your soul,'" Rabbi Akiva replied. "Do you understand what this all means? It means that you are to love Him even if He takes your very soul. Realizing this, I wondered: When shall I ever be blessed with the chance to fulfill this commandment? Now I have been so blessed. Shall I fail, then, to fulfill what I have longed to fulfill?" So he continued his prayer: "Adonai Eloheinu, Adonai Echad! The Lord our God, the Lord is One!" As the word Echad came from his lips, he drew it out, until the last breath issued from his body. At the very moment when he breathed his last, the Holy Word vibrating on his breath, a Voice resounded from Heaven, proclaiming, "Happy are you, Akiva! For your soul has departed from this world with the word Echad!" It is said when the ministering angels had witnessed the cruel death visited upon the rabbi, they gathered about the Holy One, blessed be He, and asked, "Is this to be the reward for one so faithfully devoted to Thy Torah and Law? Surely he should have been delivered by Your hand from the hands of these murderers. They should have died so, not he!" "They already have their portion in this life," the Lord answered the angels. And a Voice resounded from Heaven, proclaiming, "Happy are you, Akiva! For you are destined for a portion of life in the World to Come!"

�֍ | *The* Glory *of* Inheritance

There is the story of an old man who groaned from the depths of his heart. Doctors were sent forth and consulted. They told him that the should drink the milk of a nanny goat. And so he went out and bought a nanny goat and brought her to his place. Not many days went by and the goat disappeared. They went out to look for her but could not find her. She was gone for several days and then returned on her own, her udder full of milk that had the taste of the garden of Eden. Not just once but many times did she disappear from the house. On one occasion the old man said to his son, "My son, I want to know where she goes to get this milk that is sweeter than honey?" His son said, "Father, I have a plan." The son told his father that he would tie a chord to the goat and whenever the goat left, he would follow her. The father agreed this was a good plan. When the goat stood up, the boy followed her all the way to a cave. They walked through the cave for a long time but finally arrived at some beautiful hills just beyond the cave. There was delicious fruit everywhere and the land was flowing with milk and honey. The boy saw some passersby along the road and called out to them, "Can you please tell me, good people, where I am and what the name of this place is?" They said, "You are in the land of Israel, near Safed." The youth raised his eyes upward and declared, "Blessed be the name of the Lord, for he has brought me to the land of Israel!" He kissed the dust and sat there under a tree. In the distance, he heard someone cry out, "Come, let us greet the Sabbath Queen!" He suddenly realized that the Sabbath eve was coming and so he took a piece a paper and began to write a letter to his father. "From the corner of the earth I sing a song of joy to tell you that I have come to peace in the land of Israel. I am sitting here near Safed, the holy city, and I am overcome in its holiness. Do not ask how I got here but take the chord attached to the goat and follow him here to the promise land of Israel." The lad rolled up the piece of paper and placed the note in the goat's ear. The boy said to himself, "When she reaches my father, my father will stroke the her head and the note will fall out. Father will pick the note up and read it and follow the goat here to the land of Israel." The goat returned to the old man but he did not stroke the goats head so the note did not fall out. Rather, he cried out, "My son, my son, where are you? Would that I had died in your place my son, my son!" And so he went on weeping and mourning over his son. The old man refused all comforting and said, "I shall mourn my son, who has passed away, even as I go to the grave!" And every time he looked at the goat he would say, "Woe to the father who has exiled his son, and woe to her who drove him from the world!" And the old man could find no comfort until he sent for the butcher to slaughter the goat. The butcher came and slaughtered the goat. As they were removing the hide, a note fell out from her ear. The old man picked up the note and said, "It's my son's handwriting!" And when he had read all that his son had written to him, he clasped the note and began to weep. "Woe is me! Woe is me who steals good fortune from his own hand, and woe is the man who returns evil for good!" For many days he mourned over the goat and refused all comfort saying, "Woe is me, for I could have gone to the land of Israel in a single leap, but now I must spend the rest of my days in the torment of this exile!" Since that time, the entrance of the cave has been hidden from sight, and there is no more shortcut. And, if he has not died, the lad will bear fruit in his old age, in the peace and calm of the Land of Life.

In the Bible God promised the land to Abraham and his descendants (Gen. 12:7). God repeats the covenant with Israel concerning the land (Gen. 13:14–18) and God's eternal promise is also given to Isaac (Gen. 17:19) and then to Jacob and his descendants (Gen. 28:12–13).

How long is the land covenant valid? For a thousand generations (that's at least 40,000 years), the covenant God swore by is "an everlasting covenant" (1Ch. 16:15–17). There were conditions given with God's covenant that if Israel was not faithful, there would be judgment and exile. The whole history of Israel and the writings of the prophets demonstrate this. But the prophets also prophesized a future restoration of Israel to the land.

Israel's return to the land that we see today can only be explained as God fulfilling the words of the prophets.[1] Even the words from the prophet Yeshua the Messiah did not set aside Israel's covenant promises but confirmed them (see Rom. 15:8 and Mat. 5:17). Romans 9:4 adds that the covenant and promises still belong to the Jewish people. Rabbi Paul says, "The people of Israel — theirs is adoption as sons; theirs the divine glory, the covenants, the receiving of the law, the temple worship and the promises."

Paul further says that all who follow the Messiah are children and heirs of the promises of God (Rom. 9:6–8). Hebrews 9:15 says, "For this reason Christ is a mediator of a new covenant, that those who are called may receive the promised eternal inheritance — now that He had died as a ransom to set them free from the sins committed under the first covenant."

As God continues to establish Israel and bring Jewish descendants back to the land in the Middle East, Jesus is bringing fulfillment to all God's promises as the Messiah grants eternal life to the World to Come.[2] Jesus is the one who grants and gives eternal life.[3]

God is fulfilling His Word by not only bringing His people back to the promise land but back to their promised Messiah. Not since the first century has there ever been a generation that is seeing so many Jewish people in so many parts of the world coming to believe in Yeshua/Jesus.[4] The great "messianic secret" today is the large numbers of Jews from all over the world that are pouring into Israel for God's final outpouring of His Spirit to be fulfilled. The final border is being crossed as all of Israel will sing and dance for their salvation and destiny draws close.

❁ | *The* Glory *of* Nations

A famous Rabbi was sitting with some friends. "When I was a young man," the Rabbi said, "I was on fire. I wanted to grab everyone by the shoulders, shake them, and convince them that I had the truth. I prayed to God that I would have the wisdom and strength to change the world. "When I reached mid-life I looked back and realized I had changed no one. The world was still the same. So I prayed to God that I would be given the wisdom and strength to change those around me who needed to see the truth. "Ah, but now I am old and my prayer is much simpler. 'God,' I pray, 'at least give me the wisdom and strength to change myself." Israel is to bless all the nations. What starts with each Israelite in community reaches outward to the whole world. Nor did the Israelites look at the Torah as their own exclusive possession. "On the contrary, it was destined for all mankind, and happy the day when all the nations accepted it" (Talmud, p.62).

Even the sacrifices at the temple were intended for all of humanity. A Jewish benediction starts with these words, "Blessed art Thou, O Lord our God, King of the Universe…"[1] Although there is some diversity and differences regarding the fate of Gentiles, the door is never bolted from the inside of mainstream Judaism against Gentiles who desire admittance from pure motives.[2]

The Torah says that God is the friend of the proselyte (Deu. 10:18). There is much teaching in rabbinic Judaism that states that the Israelite and the convert were placed on the same level.[3] One Rabbi even declared, "The Holy One, blessed be He, did not exile Israel among the nations for any other reason than that proselytes should be added to them."[4]

Rabbinic Judaism teaches that the righteous from all nations and peoples will inherit the bliss of the Hereafter.[5] During the time of the Messiah, blinded eyes will be opened and nations shall come into the light. Through this last days outpouring of God's Spirit upon the face of the earth, the Hebrew Bible says, "For then will I turn to the peoples a pure language, that they may all call upon the name of the Lord, to serve Him with one consent" (Zep. 3:9).

The question of the conversion of nations is not whether it will take place but how will it take place? Daniel 8:13 and Zachariah 12:3, along with Luke 21:24, speak of the nations assaulting and trampling over Jerusalem. Daniel 12:7 reveals this shattering of God's holy people will prove salvific for the nations. Ezekiel and Daniel and the book of Revelation show a cosmic battle of pagan religion and power over and against Yahweh's power and authority. The Hebrew Scriptures point to all the nations in the end will finally acknowledge God's rule and worship Him.[6]

The universal worship of God is prophesized in Psalm 96:7–8; Isaiah 24:15–16, and 42:12. The prophets predict suffering and martyrdom for the people of God which will lead to the conversations of the nations. There is this grand reversal in the book of Revelation, whereas one sees in Esther the threat of genocide and the deliverance of God's people. In the book of Revelation, the people of God are slaughtered by the beast which leads to the conversion of their enemies.[7]

In the final period of world history, God will not deliver His faithful people by the slaughter of their enemies, as He did in the days of Moses, Elijah, and Esther. Rather, He will allow His people to be slaughtered by their enemies which will bring about repentance, faith, and the final vindication of God's people to where the whole world gives allegiance to the divine sovereignty to God.

Just as the Messiah became the sacrificial Lamb and was a faithful witness who was killed, died, and was vindicated by resurrection, so the church becomes a suffering witness which plays a crucial role in all nations coming into God's righteous Kingdom. Thus, the martyrs, the redeemed from all the nations, are offered to God as a kind of "first fruits of the harvest" for the gathering in and the "reaping" of all the nations into the Kingdom of God (Rev. 11:13; 14:14–16; 15:4).

There is a song of Moses (Exo. 15) and a new song of the Lamb in Revelation 15:2–4. There is this finale and expectation that all the nations will come to acknowledge the God of Israel and worship him. God's Kingdom will come and all kingdoms will become His! Israel and the church come together in the last prophetic word in Scripture in the New Jerusalem. The names of the twelve tribes of Israel are on its gates (Rev. 21:12), as in Ezekiel's vision (Eze. 48:30–34), while the names of the twelve apostles are on its foundation (Rev. 21:14).

All the nations worship God (Psa. 86:9; Rev. 15:4) and His Messiah (Psa. 89:27: Rev. 5). There will be a righteous "remnant" that God calls out of every nation to be included into the history of His covenant people. In the place of the idolatrous allegiance to the beast is now the spectacular glory of God (Rev. 11:13; 14:7; 15:4).

The description of the tree of life in Revelation 22:2 comes from Ezekiel 47:12. Ezekiel says the leaves are simply for healing, whereas Revelation says they are for "the healing of the nations." John in his revelation is saying that the nations who dwell in the new Jerusalem are healed from their idolatry and other sins and are translated from the kingdom of darkness into God's holy Kingdom of light.

The book of Revelation takes the human-like figure of Daniel 7:14 to be none other than Jesus Christ (Rev. 1:13; 14:14). Isaiah 66:18, "I am coming to gather all the nations and languages" is therefore fulfilled in all the kingdoms becoming the Messiah's Kingdom (Rev. 11:15).

One day the patriarch Abraham saw a man walking through the desert. He invited the traveler into his tent to dine and spend the night. Of course, the fellow eagerly accepted the hospitality. However, as Abraham was preparing the meal, he learned that his guest was a pagan. Abraham asked the man to leave without giving him so much as a fig to eat. That night God appeared to Abraham in a dream and asked, "Why did you treat your guest so poorly?" Abraham replied, "Because he did not worship you, the one true God." God said, "But Abraham, I have put up with that unbeliever for eighty years. Couldn't you have endured him for one night?"

Threads *of* Disaster *and* Deliverance

✿ | *The* Dark Thread *of* Sin

A respected woman once came to ask the advice of a Rabbi. As soon as the Rabbi saw her, he shouted, "Adulteress! You sinned only a short time ago, and yet now you have the insolence to step in this house!" Then from the depths of her heart, the woman replied, "The Lord of the world has patience with the wicked. He is in no hurry to make them pay their debts and He does not disclose their secrets to any creature, lest they be ashamed to turn to Him. In His mercy He does not hide His face from them. But the Rabbi of Apt sits there in his chair and cannot resist revealing at once what the Creator has kept secret." From that time on, the Rabbi of Apt used to say, "No one ever got the better of me except once – and then it was a woman."

The Rabbis pray this prayer to God which they believe is addressed God Himself, "May it be acceptable before Me, may it be My will, that My compassion may overcome Mine anger, and that it may prevail over My justice when My children appeal to Me, that I may deal with them in mercy and love."[1]

The Talmud teaches that man is a sinful creature who does many evil deeds over his lifetime. The Rabbi's referred to the evil side of man as the "evil impulse" that resides within man. The Rabbis cite different opinions when it comes to issues like sinless perfection and repentance even after death.[2] One Rabbi said, "If the Holy One, blessed be He, had entered into judgment with Abraham, Isaac, and Jacob, they would not have been able to stand the reproof."[3]

The Jews believed that sin affected all of creation since the fall in the Garden. Sin brings death to every creature. Even Israel's sin of the golden calf affected the destinies of mankind. The Talmud says, "There is no generation in which there is not an ounce from the sin of the

Golden Calf."[4]

The Rabbis taught that man is burdened with the consequences of sin but no Rabbi taught that man inherited sin from another in which he was not personally responsible for. The great rabbinic teachers taught man at his birth was sinless. Therefore we have the saying, "Happy the man whose hour of death is like the hour of his birth; as at his birth he is free of sin, so at his death may he be free of sin."[5]

Sin is nothing more or less than rebellion against a Holy God. Virtue is conformity to the Torah and sin is its disregard. All sin is serious before God and is a revolt against the divine will. Three sins which bring a forfeiture of life are idolatry, unchastity, and bloodshed.[6] The fourth capital sin is slander. Psalms 22:3 says, "May the Lord cut off all flattering lips, the tongue that speaketh proud things."

The Talmud also says that "the adulterer is a practical atheist" since it is deduced from Scripture, "The eye of the adulterer waiteth for the twilight, saying, 'No eye shall see me" (Job 24:15). Immodesty of speech is also severely condemned. Even those who listen to gossip or slander without protesting are condemned.

Another cardinal sin is bloodshed since it is the destruction of one created in the divine image.[7] There is a powerful quote from the Talmud that says, "If one sheds blood... it is as though he had diminished the likeness of the King."[8] Even the sin of hatred is like murder. For the very heart of following God and truth is loving God and your fellow man. The Talmud says in reference to those who built the Tower of Babel, "Since they hated one another, the Holy One, blessed is He, blotted them out from this world and the World to Come."[9]

Lying, in rabbinic thought, is equivalent to theft.[10] "There are seven classes of thieves, and the first among them all is he who steals the mind of his fellow-creatures (by lying words)." The Talmud says, "The band of liars cannot receive the presence of the *shekinah*."[11] Nor should a person who does not keep a promise even to a child in so doing teaches him falsehood.

There is much talk and strong language denouncing scoffers, hypocrites, and slanderers. There is no place for dishonesty and double-mindedness within Jewish faith. One of the painful declarations in the Talmud in regards to the history of Israel and man is "A community addicted to hypocrisy is loathsome like an unclean thing, and will be driven into exile."[12]

The greatest of all sins is the sin of causing others to sin.[13] "To make another to sin is worse than to kill him; because to murder a person is only to remove him from this world, but to cause him to sin is to exclude him from the World to Come as well."[14]

An important distinction is made in rabbinic thought between private and public sins. Sin in public is a more heinous offense but the Talmud also says, "If a man commits a transgression in secret, God will proclaim it publicly."[15] Open transgressions are treated as more serious sins in their consequences because they may lead others in following their examples.

Sin must be kept in check in its early stage or it can grow into a conformed habit. Sins build upon one another and feed each other. One Rabbi warned, "Be not wrathful and you will not sin; be not intoxicated and you will not sin."[16] Self control and character built upon understanding from God's law and ways counters the deadly force of evil and sin. The Talmud teaches, "Know what is above you — a seeing eye, and a hearing ear, and all your deeds are written in a book."[17]

The Talmud also encourages believers to keep their minds occupied with wholesome thoughts and their hands engaged in honest toil. In this way one does not find time to do sinful things. One's time is filled with doing good to others.

If sin is the spiritual disease of man then repentance is the healing medicine of the soul. The Talmud says, "Seven things were created before the world was formed. They are: Torah, repentance, Paradise, *Gehinnom* (Hell), the throne of Glory, the sanctuary, and the name of the Messiah."[18] "Great is repentance for it reaches to the Throne of Glory." For where there is repentance, the Messiah is near![19]

An old woman in the village was said to be receiving divine visions from God. The local Rabbi demanded proof of their authenticity. "When God appears to you," he said, "ask Him to tell you my sins, which are known to Him alone. That should be evidence enough." The woman returned a month later and the Rabbi asked if God had appeared to her again? She said He had. "Did you put the question to Him?" "I did " she said. "And what did he say?" The woman replied, "Tell your Rabbi I have forgotten his sins."

❀ | *The* Bright Thread *of* Salvation

Puzzled by a certain passage in the Talmud, a disciple of Rabbi Yitzchak Meir asked his teacher a question. "Rabbi," said the disciple, "the sages tell us that in Hebrew the stork is called chasidah, which means 'the pious one' or 'the loving one.' They go on to teach that the stork is referred to by this name because it offers so much love to its mate and to its offspring. Indeed, it is said that the stork brings food to the nests of other storks as well. Now if this is so, why would the Torah declare the stork to be among the unclean birds?" "You ask an excellent question," replied the rabbi. "Know that the Torah deems the stork to be unclean because it is kind only to its own and brings food only to the nests of other storks. While it offers its love to its own, the bird has no love for strangers. The Torah teaches us that those who are closest to God are the widow, the orphan, the poor, and the stranger. Why? Because these are the ones who have nowhere to turn. Therefore we must turn to them, lest God turn away from us. There is no human being, Gentile or Jew, who is not one of our own. We are all children of Adam.

God is Israel's redeemer and salvation (Exo. 15:2). From the deliverance of "the exodus" from Egyptian bondage to the deliverance and promises of the land of Canaan, God is the rock of Israel and saves her. The Psalms express the joy of salvation (13:5; 21:1; 68:19) and the salvation that God has for Israel (53:6) and for the whole earth (74:12).

Isaiah prophetically speaks of "salvation to the ends of the earth" (52:10) and the helmet of salvation on the head of God's people (59:17; also see Eph. 56:13–18). Israel can rejoice and be glad for their salvation is an "everlasting salvation" from the Lord (Isa. 45:17). Salvation in Jewish thought is the renewal of the whole creation.

Salvation and judgment are inevitably linked in Scripture from the prophets who spoke of the great and terrible "Day of the Lord" to the great and final judgment in the book of Revelation of the whole world. Jewish hope in the Messiah understood a nationalistic restoration of the Messiah's kingship and "messianic war" over all the Gentile oppressors establishing God's rule over the whole earth.[1]

The book of Revelation interestingly views Jesus as the Davidic Messiah who is "the root and descendent of David" (Isa. 11:10; Rev. 5:1; 22:16). The Messiah of David is the one who will conquer the enemies of Israel. Christ the Messiah is "the Lion of Judah" (Gen. 49:9; Rev. 5:5) that comes with a sword in His mouth (Rev. 1:16; 2:12,16; 19:21) which He will strike down the nations (19:15; see Isa. 11:4; 49:2) and judges them with righteousness (Rev. 19:11; also see Isa. 11:4).

What one sees through a series of visions in the book of Revelation is the fulfillment of God's promises in Jesus who wins His victory not by military conquest but by God's vulnerable love and power over the false kings of the earth. One also see the international community of God's people victory with the Messiah. The Messiah conquers (Rev. 3:21; 5:5; 17:14) and His people share in His victory (2:7,11,17,28; 3:5,12,21; 12:11; 15:2; 21.7). As was predicted long ago by the prophets, the Messiah has victory over all the nations (2:18,26–28; 11:15,18; 12:5,10; 14:1; 16:14,16; 19: 15).

The messianic war describes the whole process of the establishment of God's Kingdom and rule throughout the whole book of revelation. All of history comes together as Christ has won the decisive victory at the cross and vindication by the resurrection. Christ's followers are given 'the keys of the Kingdom' now to walk in authority by the same resurrection power of God's Spirit. But God's final victory still lies in the future.

Salvation in Jewish thought is not just personal but corporate, not just concerned with the World to Come but the redemption of the whole earth.[2] This Messianic "seed" grows and produces such a great harvest that heaven is full of thousands of multitudes from every tribe and nation. The promise to Abraham is ultimately fulfilled in the Messiah that Israel would indeed be a blessing to "all the nations."

There is a story from the Midrash of "Rabbi Gamaliel, Rabbi Eleazer ben Azariah, Rabbi Joshua, and Rabbi Akiba were on their way to Rome when they heard its crowd from a far distance. They all began to weep but Rabbi Akiba laughed. They said to him: These heathen peoples worship idols and live in safety and prosperity, whereas the Temple of our God is burned down and has become a dwelling place for the beasts of the field, so should we not weep?" He said to them, "For this reason am I merry. If they that offend Him fare thus, how much better shall they fare that obey Him!" On another occasion they were coming up to Jerusalem, and when they reached the Temple mount, they saw a fox emerging from the Holy of Holies. They fell down weeping, but Akiba laughed. They said to him, "Akiba, you always amaze us. Shall we not weep that the Holy of Holies a fox emerges, and concerning it the verse is fulfilled, 'For the mountain of the Zion, which is desolate, the foxes walk upon it?' He said to them: "For this reason am I merry. Behold it states, 'And I will take unto Me faithful witnesses to record, Uriah the priest, and Zechariah the son of Jeberechiah.' Now Uriah lived in the time of the first Temple, while Zechariah lived in the time of the second Temple! But what did Uriah say? "Thus saith the Lord of hosts: Zion shall be plowed as a field, and Jerusalem shall become heaps.' And what did Zechariah say? 'There shall yet old men and old women sit in the broad places of Jerusalem... And the broad places of the city shall be full of boys and girls playing.' The Holy One, blessed be He, said, 'Behold I have these two witnesses, and if the words of Uriah are fulfilled, the words of Zechariah will be fulfilled; and if the words of Uriah prove vain the words of Zechariah will prove vain.' I rejoiced because the words of Uriah have been fulfilled and in the future the words of Zechariah will be fulfilled." There upon in these terms did they address him: "Akiba, you have consoled us; may you be comforted by the coming of the herald of the redemption!"

✤ *The* Dark Thread *of* Judgment

The rabbi announced that the message that week was the arrival of the Messiah. Everyone came in expectation to hear a message concerning the Messiah. To the Rabbi and people's horror, someone had entered the building and vandalized it. Scribbled on all the walls were the words "Beware." No part of the building had been spared from these words etched on the doors, walls, and ceiling. Everywhere were the words, "Beware, beware, Beware, beware..." Everyone was shocked, confused and terrified. What were they supposed to beware of? It did not say. It just said "Beware." The first impulse of the people was to wipe out every trace of this defilement and sacrilege. They were restrained from doing this only by the thought that maybe the words were somehow from the Messiah himself. The mysterious word "Beware" began to sink into the minds of the people each time they came to synagogue. They began to beware of the Scriptures, so that they were able to profit from them without falling into bigotry. They began to beware of everything around them as a signpost to God. Even the Rabbi began to beware of his power over the people, so he was able to help without trying to control them. All the people began to beware of religion without power and any smugness that leads to self-righteousness. They became more compassionate to the weak and concerned about justice for the poor. They began to beware of prayer, beginning to struggle for searching and honest words while being less reliant upon themselves. The people have now inscribed the shocking word over the entrance of their building so that no one forget or ever take for granted the holiness and certain coming judgment of God.

The Scriptures portray God as a holy, just God. God rewards the righteous and punishes the wicked. When it comes to the justice and judgment of God, the Rabbis said, "We may not question the decisions of Him Who spake and the world came into being; but He judges all in truth and everything in accordance with strict justice."[1]

God's measure is sure and exacts measure with measure. An illustration of this would be how the Egyptians tried to destroy Israel by water (drowning their sons in the Nile river) whereas God punished them by drowning them in the depths of the water of the Red Sea. Samson also went after the lust of his eyes and his retribution was the Philistines plucked his eyes out. Absalom in his pride and vain glory in his hair was caught and destroyed by his hair.

The Rabbis recognized the problem of prosperity among the wicked and the suffering of the righteous. The mystery of evil and suffering is only known in the mind of God. For God tests everyone, especially His own.[2]

A strong belief among Jews is the cardinal belief of retribution. No matter how justice was or was not dealt with on earth, there will always be a "day of reckoning" in the World to Come. The Talmud says, "The Lord of Hosts will be exalted in judgment" (Isa. 5:16).[3] The whole image of God on a throne is a throne of judgment.[4]

The Talmud says that "God has ordained the day of the Great Judgment which will take place after death… The Israelites say, "Blessed be He Who formed you in judgment, Who nourished you in judgment, sustained you in judgment, and gathered you in judgment, and will hereafter raise you in judgment."[5]

No one will escape the Great Judgment of God but all people will stand before the blessed Holy God of Israel. The Talmud says God has made *Gehinnom* (Hell) for the wicked and *Gan Eden* (Heaven) for the righteous.[6] They both posses a final and eternal dwelling place.

For the condemned, the wicked will murmur against God and say:

"Lo, we looked for His salvation, and such a fate should befall us!" He answers them, "When you were on earth did you not quarrel and slander and do all kinds of evil? Were you not responsible for strife and violence? That is what is written, "Behold, all ye that kindle a fire, that gird yourselves about with firebrands. That being so, "Walk ye in the flame of your fire and among the brands that ye have kindled."[7]

The Talmud also lists seven classes or levels of *Gan Eden*.[8] In preparation for the day of judgment a record of everything people have done on earth is kept written in a book. Even if many of the deeds are good, the only question that counts ultimately is "the fear of the Lord your treasure?"[9]

Jewish thought teaches that the soul is rejoined to the body for the purpose of judgment.[10] Although there are diversity of interpretations within rabbinic teachings concerning the fate of the wicked, eternal punishment is taught by some of the Rabbis. For example, the Talmud says:

> But now, when I am being led into the presence of the King of Kings, the Holy One, blessed be He, Who lives and endures for all eternity, Who if He be wrathful against me His anger is eternal, Who if He imprisoned me the imprisonment would be everlasting, Who if He condemned me to death the death would be forever... when before me lie two ways, one of Gan Eden, and the other Gehinnon, and I know not to which I am being led — shall I not weep?[11]

There is this beautiful image in Jewish thought of the bride and the bridegroom. The Talmud says, "Does a bridegroom prepare a banquet for guests and not sit with them... The Holy One, blessed be He... enters the garden and says, "I am come into My garden, My sister, My bride."[12] The whole rabbinic tradition of heaven and hell parallels the great universal judgment that comes in the book of Revelation.[13]

The book of Revelation gives three series of judgments: the seven seal-openings (6:1–17; 8:1,3–5) the seven trumpets (8:2,6–21; 11:14–19) and the seven bowls (15:1,5–21). The seventh (final and complete number) of each series portrays the final act of judgment in which evil is destroyed and God's Kingdom arrives.

God's judgment is final, retributive, true and just (16:7; 19:2; 15:3) and God is holy, true, and sovereign (15:4). There is a progression of severity in God's judgments. The judgments of the seal openings affect a quarter of the earth (6:8) those of the trumpets affect a third of the earth (8:7–12; 9:18), but those of the bowls are universal.

The plagues in the book of Revelation are modeled after the plagues of Egypt. The judgments in Revelation 16–19 are aimed at destroying the systems of the world — political, economic, and religious which oppose God and His ways. There is a grim picture of slaughter in chapter 19:18–19 where those who follow the beast, Babylon, and evil kings are destroyed. The day of judgment is also a day of vindication of God's people as every knee will bow one day before the victorious Messiah.

❀ | *The* Bright Thread *of* Righteousness

One day Rabbi Yochanan ben Zakkai gathered his disciples around him and said to them, "I have a very important task for you. I want you to go out into the world and search out the ways of men to see what is truly good in humanity. Then return to me and tell me what you have found." As always, the disciples obeyed their teacher. They walked among people of every class and occupation, every background and lot in life. After a time, when each believed that he had found what was truly good in people, they returned to the rabbi to report what they had learned. "So tell me," said Rabbi Yochanan, first addressing Rabbi Eliezer. "What have you found to be truly good?" "A good eye," Eliezer replied. "For those who have a good eye have an eye for suffering of others. So they are led to be generous." "Well said," the teacher nodded. "And you, Rabbi Yehoshua, what have you found to be truly good?" "A good friend," he answered. "A man should not only cultivate a good friend but should himself be a good friend. That is how life takes on value. For a friend has no price and is more precious than gold." "You too have spoken well," the rabbi answered. Then turning to Rabbi Yose, he asked, "What have you learned?" "I have learned," said Yose, "that a good neighbor is truly good. A man cannot live in isolation from others but needs company in order to be truly good. It is from a good neighbor that we learn how to be a good neighbor." "We all may learn from what you have learned," Rabbi Yochanan commented. "But I wonder what Rabbi Shimon has found to be truly good?" "I have found that the person who looks ahead and attends to the consequences of his actions is truly good," said Rabbi Shimon. "Our deeds create angels for good or for evil, and the angels we create go out into the world to do good or evil. Thus our every move, our every thought, disturbs all the universe and affects human lives." "What you say is profound," said Rabbi Yochanan. "Listen well, all of you, to Rabbi Shimon. But we have not heard from Rabbi Eleazer ben Arach." The disciples and their teacher turned to Rabbi

Eleazer, prepared to listen to his discourse on what is truly good in humanity. But all he said was: "A good heart is truly good." At this their teacher smiled and declared, "I prefer the words of Eleazer ben Arach to all of your words combined. In his words are contained your words. A good heart sees rightly and seeks out other human beings, loving our neighbor, as the Torah commands us. And a good heart looks not only ahead but also above, loving God, as the Torah commands us. Yes, Rabbi Eleazer has spoken well."

The whole Jewish faith is a religion of God's grace and a heart after God. The Talmud says, "The difference between the righteous and the wicked is defined in this way, 'The wicked are under the control of their heart (which is evil), but the righteous have their hearts under (God's) control.'"[1]

Another way to sum up the law and the prophets is where the Talmud says, "He who is good toward God and his fellow-men is the righteous man who is good; but one who is good toward God and evil toward his fellow-men is not good."[2]

The Messiah taught that blessed are the pure in heart for they will see God (Mat. 5:8). When we treasure God over everything else, there one will find a righteous heart made clean by God. The Messiah summed it up like this, "But seek first the Kingdom of God and His righteousness and all these things shall be added to you" (Mat. 6:33).

A wealthy rabbi longed to take up residence in a city of righteousness. His children were growing up very rapidly, as children do, and he wanted his family to live in a place that would be good for their souls. In order to find just the right city, he hired several emissaries and sent them to various places in order to see whether or not they might be places where he and his family would want to live. To each of these investigators the rabbi gave a large sum of money for expenses. He was willing to spend whatever it took in order to dwell among the righteous. The first man that the rabbi sent forth arrived in the city assigned to him and immediately took room in a plush and costly inn. Rather than seek out the sages of the city or even meet with its common citizens, he squandered his money on the city's night life. Soon he fell in with a group of shady characters, who ended up stealing his money from him. Now penniless, the investigator returned to the rabbi and reported, "The city to which you sent me is full of evil. There are thieves and cutthroats everywhere. I tell you, it's a regular Sodom!" The man denounced the city in such extreme terms that the rabbi wondered whether what he said about it could possibly be true. Therefore he sent a second investigator to explore the same city. When the rabbi's emissary arrived, he found a modest room in an equally modest inn and went immediately to the local synagogue. He was a man devoted to God, and it was time for the afternoon prayers. In the synagogue he found numerous people in worship, and after their prayers many of them invited him into their homes. "Please do me the honor, sir, of sitting at my table," said one. "Let me offer you a place of comfort to rest from your journey," said another. "I would like for you to meet my family," offered a third. "One who is new to the city should not have to be alone." "When the man returned to the rabbi to make his report, he declared, "I have found the perfect city for you, Rabbi. It is filled with righteous people who treat strangers with lovingkindness." While the rabbi was pleased to hear this, he was also rather puzzled over having received such conflicting reports about the same city. Unable to resolve the puzzle, he decided to go to the city and see for himself what was there. Before long he understood. Upon his return he gathered together the two men he had sent out and said, "I understand now why each of you has returned from the same city with such different impressions of it. It is because one of you is wicked, while the other is good. Those who are wicked seek wickedness, and they inevitably find it. But those who are good seek what is good, and that is what they find. I am in your debt more than you know. For you have taught me that we find not only what we seek — we find what we are. And so there is no need for me to move my family to another city. I need only move my soul closer to the good."

The Dance *of* Faith

The Family Dance

There once was a man who had an adolescent son who had fallen into sinful ways. The boy would stay out all night, carousing with the Gentiles, and chasing after girls. He even spoke to his mother and father with disrespect. Finally, at a complete loss as to how he might lead his son back to the proper path, the father went to speak to the Baal Shem Tov. "Rabbi," he said, "I am at my wits end. My son has fallen into such evil that I fear for his soul. He has completely abandoned the teachings of our faith, and his behavior is disgraceful. I have threatened to beat him or to throw him out of the house, but nothing seems to work. How can I convince him to change his ways?" "Love him more," the Baal Shem replied. "But he deserves no love!" the father answered. "That is all the more reason to increase your love for him," the Baal Shem insisted. "Do you think God loves us because we deserve it? No. Love is the very essence of life. It is the light that illuminates the path to God. If you would have your son follow that path, then you must be such a light unto him. Love him more."

The whole basis for Jewish social life and relationships is the family. The family's devotion, relationships, worship, and spiritual life is cultivated in one's family. The purpose of marriage was to raise and train children in the ways of Torah. Middle-Eastern culture is a honor and shame culture and it was imperative to honor one's family in all that one does.

The Talmud says that women are equal to men and are in no way inferior to men.[1] A woman's role and activity may be different than a man but she played no less significance in the welfare and growth of family and community life. The Talmud says, "Scripture places men and women on an equality with regard to all the laws of the Torah."[2]

There is a rabbinic saying that goes like this:

> *With respect to the formation of woman from a rib we have this reason for the choice: 'God considered from which part of man to create a woman. He said, I will not create her from the head that she should not hold up her head too proudly; nor from the eye that she should not be too curious; nor from the ear that she should be an eavesdropper; nor from the mouth that she should be too talkative; not from the heart that she should be too jealous... but I made her from the part of the body which is hidden that she should be modest.*[3]

Marriage is sacred and holy and "when a husband and wife are worthy, the *shekinah* is with them."[4] The Jewish family is all about honoring one another whether that be in marriage or children honoring parents or bringing honor to one's family. Although the husband was the head or authority of the house, a wife is to be greatly valued and a Mother is so respected that one Rabbi said, "When he heard the footsteps of his Mother, he exclaimed, "I stand up before the *Shekinah*."[5]

God's laws are to be respected in all things, especially the commandment of honoring one's parents. Not only is a person to honor his mother and father in life but even in death. Even the memories of parents should honor God as it honors them.

In the first century there were two schools of thought that took opposite views of the biblical text when it came to the issue of divorce. The school of Shammie understood Deu. 24:1 which speaks of a man sending his wife away if he hath found some un-seemingly thing in her to mean he may not divorce her unless she has been unfaithful to him.[6] The school of Hillel on the other hand, understood the phrase to mean a man could divorce his wife for almost anything, "even if she burnt the dinner."[7]

Men in biblical times could initiate a divorce but a woman could only do so with her husband's consent. One could remarry after death but not for desertion. It was forbidden to divorce a woman who goes insane. The reason for this was she would be deprived of a protector and could easily fall prey to an evil-minded person. Although there was diversity and latitude in how some of these issues were handled, the concern for justice and doing what was right at the heart of these decisions.

Children are to be regarded as precious gifts on loan from God and should be guarded and faithfully and lovingly cared for. The proverb, "Blessed is he that doeth righteousness at all times" was understood by some in the Talmud to refer to the one who nourishes his children while they are young.[8] Moderation, even handedness, no partiality, and responsible discipline were guidelines in training a child in the way of the Lord.

The principal responsibility of parents was to educate their children as members of the community of Israel. Children are to be taught the Torah and even the orphan and the poor were to be given a Torah-based education. The Jewish way of life so highly valued children and their education that one proverb says, "A city in which there are no school children will suffer destruction."[9]

Jews and Christians are to faithfully provide for their families.[10] Although families may even betray us (see Mat. 10:21; Mark 13:12; Luke 21:16,17), the Messiah will never betray us. Allegiance to God and His Messiah is even over family commitment and responsibilities (see Luke 14:26; Mat. 8:21–22).

Jesus is God's natural born son, but we become sons of God by adoption (Rom. 8:15). Natural family members are a precious gift from God but the Messiah even sets that in its proper place next to the spiritual family that God calls all people to be members of His agape community (Mat. 12:48 49; Luke 8.21). The Messiah said, "My mother and brothers are those who hear God's word and put it into practice." The Jewish and Christian community are to be faithful Torah-based communities consisting of families led by God's Spirit.

✿ | *The* Dance *of* Friendship

There was a father who pledged to give each of his ten children an inheritance of one hundred golden coins. He was wealthy when he made the promise, but as he neared the end of his life, money was in short supply. Eventually it became apparent he would be unable to fulfill his promise. Hours before his death, the father called his children to his bedside. He began to give each of the children the money he pledged. To each of the first nine, he was able to fulfill his word, giving them one hundred gold coins. But when it was time to pay his youngest daughter, he requested that the other children leave the room. "My daughter," the father said, "I am unable to give you one hundred gold coins. Here, you may have twenty coins, for it is all that remains." At once the daughter protested, "But Father, if you knew you would be unable to give one hundred coins, why didn't you adjust the amounts you gave to the other nine?" "Better that I should fulfill my word to as many of my children as possible," the father said. "However, I have something of far greater value than gold which I give in place of the coins. I offer you my ten best friends. Their love and support has been worth more to me than all the gold in the world. As a final request, I would ask you treat these friends well." And with that word, the father died. Now it happened that the other nine children immediately took a liking to their wealth. Some brought houses, some land. Others left on extended vacations. The youngest daughter stayed at home with her twenty gold coins and grew more and more despondent. One day, however, she remembered her father's request, and decided to invite her father's friends to an extravagant dinner. She spent her entire inheritance on the invitations, the dinner, and on bottles of fine wine. When her father's friends arrived, she gave each of them a seat of honor, provided entertainment, and made certain that each had his fill of good food. After the dinner the ten friends said to one another, "Of all the children, the youngest daughter is the only one who has displayed the integrity of her father. Let us return the kindness." And so it was that each of the ten friends gave the daughter one hundred gold coins, thus fulfilling the saying, "Friendship is more valuable than gold."

The Torah centers on brotherly love "Thou shall love thy neighbor as thyself" (Lev. 19:18). All people the Scriptures says are created in the image of God and are descended from one ancestor or common origin. The Rabbis were not just merely concerned with the relationship between people and their maker, but also their relationship with their neighbors and friends. Proverbs 3:4 says, "So that thou shall find favor and good understanding in the sight of God and man." Jewish thought is forged in community and togetherness with others. There is a strong prophetic tradition for even foreigners, aliens, and strangers to be treated justly and become friends.[1]

Rabbinic thought sees a dynamic relationship between individuals and the community. One cannot exist separately-but-interdependently with one another. There is a story in the Talmud that says:

It is like a company of men on board a ship. One of them took a drill and began to bore a hole under him. The other passengers said, "What are you doing?" He replied, "Am I not making a hole under my seat?" They retorted, "But the water will enter and drown us all!"[2]

The fabric of individual identity and communal solidarity are so interconnected that God created us for neighborly love and for even strangers to become friends.

All social relationships are to be done with love, justice, and compassion in mind. Scripture says, "Two are better than one" (Ecc. 4:9). Even when one reads the Torah should acquire a friend for himself to read the Scriptures with him, to read the Talmud with him, drink with him, and disclose secrets to him.[3] Friends keep each other accountable and will tell each other the truth. A fascinating rabbinic story is about how Aaron's relationships and friendships are transformed by holiness and righteousness.

When Aaron walked along the street and met a wicked man, he gave him a greeting. The next day, when that person wanted to commit a transgression, he would say to himself, 'How can I, after doing such an act, lift up my eyes and look at Aaron? I should feel ashamed before him who gave me a greeting.' As a consequence he would refrain from doing wrong. Similarly, when two men were at enmity with each other, Aaron would visit one of them and say to him, 'My son, see how your friend is behaving; he beats his breasts, he tears his garment, and cries, 'Woe to me, how can I look in to the face of my friend? I am ashamed before him since it was I who acted so shabbily towards him!' Aaron would continue to sit with him until he had banished all enmity from his heart. Then he went and spoke exactly the same words to the other party until he had removed all enmity from him. The result was that when the two men met they embraced and kissed each other.[4]

Friendship starts with charity that begins at home and runs towards the least and serving the poor. Love not only puts others first but puts friendship before one's own needs. Friendship and charity starts at home where hospitality and even the *shekinah* of God resides because God continually brings peace, hope, and love in relationships.

Balance and moderation also brings harmony to relationships. Everything is to be done in joy and trembling of the Lord. Benevolent love and risky self-denial may even turn the wicked or an enemy into a friend in the end.

Abraham was called God's friend (2Ch. 20:7). God's friendship with us transforms all relationships. The Messiah will even turn those who are deemed servants into friends (John 15:15–16).

A man went into the woods to hunt, but lost his way. For days he wandered in the forest, disoriented and confused, desperately trying to find his way out. After some time, he saw another man approaching in the distance. His hopes soared. "At last," he thought to himself, "a person who knows how to get out of this forest." When they met, he asked the man, "My brother, can you tell me the way out of this forest? I have been wandering for days, but have been unable to find the way." The other fellow answered, "Brother, I do not know the way out either. I, too, have been wandering about these woods for days. But this much I can tell you — do not go the way I have gone. I know for certain that it does not lead out. Let us journey together. Perhaps, side by side, we can figure a way out."

The Dance *of* Humility

In the pursuit of righteousness, a disciple of Rabbi Nachum of Stephanesht once went to his teacher with a question. "Can you tell me, Rabbi," he asked, "what piety is?" "You raise a very good question," the Rabbi replied. "I have thought long and hard about this matter, for you to know that my father, Rabbi Yisrael of Rizhin, never spoke of it. I do not know what piety is, but I think I know what it can become. It seems to me that piety may be a kind of cloak with which the self-righteous conceal themselves. It is something pleasing to the eye that they parade before others and before themselves, never mindful of the eye of God that looks on and sees through every artifice." But the material of this cloak is made of arrogance, for only the arrogant would stoop to raising themselves above their fellow human beings. Its lining consists of grudges, for the self-righteous go through life feeling cheated by a world that had not given them their due. And it is sewn with threads of bitterness and dejection, for piety of this sort always comes at the price of rejoicing in life." "But how do we seek righteousness, as the Torah commands us to do?" the student replied. "Seek righteousness," said the Rabbi, "by seeking humility, gratitude, and joy. Seek righteousness by serving others. True righteousness lies in the realization that our fellow human beings open up what is more than we are, what is better than we are. It lies not in hiding behind the cloak of piety but in moving into the openness of humility."

The humble person handles the presence of others with gentle hands, a soft heart, and an unveiled mind. God can be God in our lives because we have relieved ourselves of the ordeal of being God. Humility is the heart response that knows ourselves as God knows us.

There is an old rabbinic saying: "A man should carry two stones in his pocket. On one is inscribed, 'I am but dust and ashes.' On the other,

'For my sake was the world created.'" The foundation of all humanity and community finds it substance in God-created humility.

The Talmud says that "humility is the greatest of all virtues."[1] I love the old rabbinic story where the Rabbis are asked the question:

> *"Who will be a son in the world to come?" They answered, "He who is meek and humble, walks about with a lowly demeanor, studies the Torah constantly, and takes no credit to himself."*

Jewish teaching persistently says that a humble mind and a lowly spirit are the attributes of children of Abraham. Even for the students of the Torah, small mindedness and humility is what leads to knowledge and true greatness.

Humility is even what attracts the *shekinah* presence of God. The Talmud says, "Scripture informs us that whoever is humble finally causes the *sheckinah* to dwell with man upon earth; and whoever is arrogant defiles the earth and causes the *sheckinah* to depart."[2]

God is looking for humble hearts for His Spirit to take up residence there. Pride and arrogance drives God's Spirit away. "Whoever is possessed of an arrogant spirit, the Holy One, blessed be He, says, I and He cannot dwell in the world together."[3]

Humility is the posture of listening to one who is greater than oneself. When we refuse to listen to God or others, then the only sound one hears is one's own voice. Solitude, listening, Sabbath-wonder, and humility all run together like streams that merge together into a mighty river.

> *Someone asked a Rabbi once, "How shall I experience the oneness of creation?" The Rabbi answered, "By listening." The student pressed the point, "But how am I to listen?" The Rabbi said, "Become an ear that pays attention to every single thing the universe is saying. The moment you hear something you yourself are saying, stop."*

Humility is the pathway towards wisdom. One of the supreme books of wisdom literature is the book of Job. Job honestly cries out, "Remember, O God, that my life is but a breath" (7:7). The book of Job deals with such heart-breaking realism with no false humility, no flowery pretenses, no pretending to posses any greater faith than we really have, but rather gut-wrenching, soul-searching, trust-giving faith in God no matter what!

As soon as we start looking down on others, we have missed the breadth and depth of mercy that God has given to our own life. The secret of Job's blamelessness that even scandalized his friends was Job had nothing to hide. Job hides nothing and therefore has nothing more to lose.

Spiritual growth is to grow in childlikeness. "To grow up is to grow down."[4] And once one beholds the face of a King, one is changed forever. The *shekinah* glory of God can not stay hidden for long. One therefore comes back to the beginning again and finds that "Wherever you find God's grandeur, you find His humility."[5]

God hates pride but gives grace to the humble. It is the humble who will cross over from death to life, from mediocrity to the greatest of being a servant of all. Even the Messiah lifts up the lowly and redeems the despised. God will one day pull away the veil and all those who poor in spirit and meek will inherit the earth.

There once lived a man so godly that even the angels rejoiced at the sight of him. But, in spite of his great holiness, he had no notion that he was holy. He just went about his humdrum tasks, diffusing goodness the way flowers unselfconsciously diffuse their fragrance and streetlights their glow. His holiness lay in this — that he forgot each person's past and looked at them as they were now, and he looked beyond each person's appearance to the very center of their being, where they were innocent and blameless and too ignorant to know what they were doing. Thus he loved and forgave everyone he met — and he saw nothing extraordinary in this, for it was the result of his way of looking at people. One day an angel said to him, "I have been sent to you by God. Ask for anything you wish and it will be given to you. Would you wish to have the gift of healing?" "No" said the man, "I'd rather God did the healing himself." "Would you want to bring sinners back to the path of righteousness?" "No" he said, "it is not for me to touch human hearts. That is the work of angels." "Would you like to be such a model of virtue that people will be drawn to imitate you?" "No," he said, "for that would make me the center of attention." "What then do you wish for?" asked the angel. "The grace of God," was the man's reply. "having that, I have all I desire." "No, you must ask for some miracle," said the angel, "or one will be forced on you." "Well, then I shall ask this: let good be done through me without my being aware of it." So it was decreed that the holy man's shadow would be endowed with healing properties whenever it fell behind him. So everywhere his shadow fell — provided he had his back to it — the sick were healed, the land became fertile, fountains sprang to life, and color returned to the faces of those who were weighed down with sorrow. But the saint knew nothing of this because the attention of people was so centered on the shadow that they forgot about the man. And so his wish that good be done through him and he forgotten was abundantly fulfilled.

The Dance *of* Sacrifice

Once there lived a widow who had an only son. One day this son was killed in a tragic accident. Beaten down with grief, the woman mourned her son's loss day and night, and no one was able to comfort her. Finally, a friend took the woman to a mysterious rabbi. "I have reached the end of my rope!" the woman cried. "I beg you to plead with the Almighty that my son might be brought back to life, so that God might at least lighten my grief." "I know a remedy for grief," the rabbi told her. "Bring me a mustard seed from a house which has never known grief. God will use this magic seed to remove the sorrow from your life."At once the woman set out to find the magic seed. She first visited the home of a wealthy family, thinking, "Surely the rich are secure from tragedy and hardship. A family such as this has known no sorrow." After knocking on the door of the mansion, the widow explained to the woman of the house why she had come. "I am in search of a home that has known no sorrow," she said, "Is this the place? If so, I beg you to give me a mustard seed." When the woman of the house heard this, she burst into tears. "Have I ever known sorrow? Oh, you have come to the wrong house!" And she proceeded to tell the widow of all the tragedies and travails her family had endured. She even invited the widow into her home to listen to all of her heartaches, and the widow stayed on for several days, listening to all these troubles and caring for the woman of the house. Afterwards, the widow continued her search, visiting many modest homes in the valley. But wherever she turned, the stories were much the same. Everyone, from the richest to the poorest, recounted tales of sadness and woe. And each time, the widow stayed behind in the home to listen and care for the needs of others. After several months, she grew used to hearing about the sorrows of others that she forgot about her own problems and her search for the magic mustard seed, never realizing that her care for others had driven the sorrow from her life.

Sacrificial living and giving and offering sacrifices to God for atonement for sin are essential teachings of Judaism. The Talmud says, "Sacrifices only atoned for the one who sinned in error, but righteousness and justice atone for him who sins either in error or intentionally... Sacrifices are only offered in this world, but righteousness and justice must be done in this world and the World to Come."[1]

The centrality of sacrifice and sanctification put the temple as the focal point of Jewish life and worship. The temple was the place of God's dwelling on earth. The authoritative Scripture scrolls were kept in the temple and its religious significance was so great that Simon the Just, high priest, 200 BC said, "On three things does the world stand: on the Torah, on the temple service, and on the deeds of loving kindness."[2] In early Jewish thought, the temple and its atoning sacrifices were indispensable to Israel's relationship to God.

The prophets strongly taught that the sacrifices by God's people without mercy and justice were meaningless without repentance and contrite hearts. But it would be a mistake to think that the prophets rejected Israel's sacrificial system. It was precisely because the sacrifices were so important and meaningful to Israelites religious practices that the prophets had to remind the people that sacrifices had no atoning power apart from devoted and repentant hearts.

Sacrifices are described in the Scriptures as a pleasing aroma to God (Gen. 8:21; Exo. 29:18, 25,41). God took pleasure in Israel's sacrifices when they were combined with devoted hearts and hearts dedicated to justice. The very reason God called His people out of Egypt was for them to offer sacrifices to him (Exo. 5:3).[3]

The annual "day of atonement" was to be made with the blood of the atoning sacrifice for sin for generations to come (see Exo. 30:10; Lev. 16:14–16,18–19).[4] When the Psalmist or the prophets speak about Israel's problem with their sacrifices, the problem was not the sacrifices and offerings themselves but their sin problem. Sin spoils everything including making Israel's sacrifices to the Lord unacceptable.

The Scriptures deal with the use and abuses of the sacrificial system. The prophets challenges were not for Israel to give up their sacrifices but to give up their evil ways. Even when the temple was destroyed, ancient rabbis instituted prayers for the restoration of the temple.[5] Both Ezra and Nehemiah risked their lives to rebuild the temple because the scandal of no temple and God's judgment on Israel was too horrible beyond description.

Beyond our sacrifices, what God really wants is our own life, our devotion, our complete surrender to Him as Lord as opposed to the mere offering of a sacrifice. Romans 12:1 says it this way, "I urge you brothers, in view of God's mercy, to offer your bodies as living sacrifices, holy and pleasing to God — this is your spiritual act of worship." Other offerings were such things as burnt offerings representing complete devotion to the Lord as well as thanksgiving offerings, and peace offerings were offered for worshipful communion.

Since the temple has been destroyed for the past nineteen hundred years, either God has left Israel without a means of atonement or He has provided it once and for all through the Messiah.[6] One can see the parallels to the righteous sufferer dying for His people in Isaiah which is fulfilled in the Messiah Yeshua/Jesus. There is in Jewish thought the concept of the death of the righteous that atones for Israel and all the nations.[7] The Zohar, the most sacred book of Jewish mysticism says, "As long as Israel dwelt in the Holy Land, the rituals and the sacrifices they performed [in the temple] removed all those diseases from the world; now the Messiah removes them from the children of the world."

First Peter 3:18 says, "for [the Messiah] died for sins once for all, the righteous for the unrighteous, to bring you to God." The Talmud and earliest rabbis teach over-and-over that "the death of the righteous will make atonement."[8] Zachariah and Ezekiel speak of a future time when Israel will be restored, as well as the temple. Just as sacrifices were offered for almost forty years after Jesus' death and resurrection (see Acts 21:17–26; Messianic Jews apparently participated in some of these sacrificial rites), could it be that sacrifices will be offered in a future temple?[9]

❁ *The* Priest's Dance

The Holy Jew, Rabbi Yaakov Yitzchak of Przysucha, once recalled to his disciples how his father would study the prayer book with him. "Not only did we examine the words," he said, "we pondered every letter of every word. One letter in particular caught my eye. It is hardly a letter at all, you see, little more than a dot. It is the letter yud. Unlike most of the other letters, two yuds were often written together, side by side. My father explained to me that two yuds formed a very special word: the holy name of God. "But what if one yud is written above another? Does that spell the holy name? "No," my father told me when I asked him, 'it does not. Written above the other, two dots indicate an interruption, a break in the speech.' "Suddenly I realized that through these letters that form His name God teaches us something very important, something that, indeed, the sages teach us. When two Jews — two Yuden — are gathered together to study Torah, face to face and on the same level, the Shekinah, God's indwelling Presence, is there also. But whenever one places himself above the other, taking to himself to be better than the other, God is absent. All that remains is a terrible emptiness. "Therefore learn how to say 'you' to your fellow Jew. For in saying 'you' to our fellow Jew, we say, 'You' to the Holy One Himself."

The whole purpose of the priesthood was to represent Israel before God at the Sanctuary (2Ch. 29:11; 35:2). The priests' responsibilities were to preserve the people through ceremonial purity so that God's presence would stay with them and bless them and other nations.

The word "priest" literally means one who "stands up in the presence of God." A priest was a man of "blessings." He was the one admitted into the holy place with sacred objects and was charged to make the offerings of atonement for the sins of the people.

According to Deuteronomy, Moses gave the Law to the Levites to keep in the Ark of the Covenant and He commanded them and the elders of Israel to "proclaim this law in the ears of the whole of Israel."[1] After their return from Exile, Malachi says, "The lips of the priest are to preserve knowledge and it is from his mouth that instruction is to be sought; he is a messenger of the Lord of Hosts" (2:7).

The priests and their worship in the temple was to be "consecrated" because of the holiness of God. The priests also established God's name of ownership upon the people through words of blessing (Num. 6:7). God's divine blessing upon his people produced wholeness and peace.

God is not an abstract idea within Jewish worship, but the all-powerful presence who moves people's hearts in both wonder and fear; unrestrained gratitude and the overwhelming desire to hide. The priests were mediators who helped establish communication and the people's life-giving relationship with God.

Not only were the Levites called as a "family" to be priests, but there would be a day when all of God's people would function as priests in God's Kingdom.[2] When Israel obeyed God's law and covenant, then God's glory would radiate through them to the whole world. Israel would fulfill God's word of being a blessing to all the nations (Gen. 22:18).

The family is so central to Jewish worship and life that God chose the tribe of Levi to be totally consecrated to the service of the sanctuary. The Levites were priests whose "sanctification" is described in detail in the Law of Moses (Exo. 29). They would purify themselves through ritual baths, sacred garments, and sacrifices of atonement and consecration. The Levites were commanded not to touch anything unclean or impure, not to approach a corpse, and not even to go into mourning (Lev. 21).

The priests administered the sacrifices and took care of the temple chores but even the holiest area (the holy of holies) was an area forbidden to them. This area was open only to a single person, the high priest, and to him on one day only, the Day of Atonement (Lev. 16). On that day, the blood of animal sacrifices was sprinkled on the "Mercy Seat" as the people's plea of forgiveness and restoration before a Holy God.[3]

The whole priesthood was about the possibility of living in communion with God and in communion with the rest of humanity. The Messiah Yeshua was understood to be the last great prophet, but He was not from the line of priests. And yet, the Messiah came to restore people into a right relationship with God and to one another. One sees how Yeshua/Jesus challenged people's views of holiness, which for him had more to do with welcoming strangers and outcasts than separating oneself from them.

The Gospel of John says that Jesus "drove out of the Temple the sheep and the cattle." That is to say, the animals that were to be offered in sacrifice. One can see a connection here to the prophecy of Malachi who said, "Suddenly the Lord whom you are seeking will enter His sanctuary... He is like a refiner's fire... He will purify the songs of Levi... "[4]

Jesus is "the Anointed One of Israel" who is the royal Messiah who fulfills David's and the prophet's words.[5] Moses words in Exodus 19:5–6 of Israel and God's people being a "kingdom of priests" is fulfilled in the Messianic community of Jesus. God is building a "spiritual house" as well as a priestly people (1Pe. 2:2–4, 9).

As God's people become the Temple of God where God's Spirit resides, communion with God is taken in these "last days" into its greatest fulfillment as God draws all people into His Holy Kingdom. We find ourselves "in the Messiah... being built together into a dwelling of God in the Spirit" (Eph. 2:21–22).

Rabbi Paul also draws upon his rich Jewish heritage and compares the priestly service in the Temple to the ministry of the gospel:

> Do you not know that those who perform the sacred rites draw their livelihood from the Temple, that those who serve the alter share with the alter? In the same way, the Lord has ordained that those who proclaim the Gospel are to live by the gospel. (1Cor. 9:13–14)

Even the earliest Jewish Christians participated in the Jewish feasts, temple services, and the great Day of Atonement (Acts 2:46; 6:7; etc.). The book of Revelation repeatedly speaks of God in Christ making His people into a kingdom of priests in fulfillment of Moses' words and bringing them to maturity as God's people (Rev. 1:6; 5:10; 20:6). The book of Hebrews says the Messiah is our High Priest and all believers are called into an intercessory priestly ministry with him. The Messiah calls His followers to be priests to one another before a Holy God (chs. 8–10).

❊ *The* Prophet's Dance

One day, as the prophet Jeremiah was engaged in the study of the mystical book of creation, a heavenly voice resounded from above, saying , "Find yourself a companion." Understanding this to mean that he was to create for himself a living being, Jeremiah sought out his son Sira to help him in the task. For three years they sat together and studied the Book of Creation in order to learn the secrets of bringing dead matter to life. After years of laboring they finally managed to transform a mass of clay into a man. Then Jeremiah heard a voice from above, "What have you done?" I have created you in my image and you have taken the secret of that image and created an image of a man Now people will say, "There is no God in the world other than those two makers of men!" Jeremiah repented and said, "What can I do to reverse the terrible thing we have done?" God told him, "Meditate what you have learned from reverse and reverse the process." Jeremiah and Sira did as the Lord instructed them and the clay man they had formed turned into dust and ashes before their very eyes. Jeremiah said to his son Sira, "I now realize that man must never engage in an activity that belongs to God alone. Our purpose in delving into the secrets of God's creative name is not to imitate God in the creation of a man-like being, but so that we may become men by assuming within ourselves and in our actions the image of God."

It is a dangerous thing to hear a word from God much less discern it correctly. The whole history of the Jewish people is hearing from God who spoke through certain individuals that the Scriptures call "prophets." The Talmud says that "Prophecy is the ability to interpret the will of God, is the effect of which the Holy Spirit is the cause."[1]

    The Talmud further explains that Isaac gave Jacob a second blessing:

...because he saw by the Holy Spirit that his descendants would be exiled among the nations of the world... The question why Jacob wept when he kissed Rachel is answered: 'He saw by the Holy spirit that he would not be buried by her side... By the aid of the Holy Spirit Moses foresaw that Israel would be oppressed by heathen powers.[2]

The Jewish people looked for the time when "Every prophet only prophesied for the days of the Messiah and the penitent."[3] The rabbinic writings looked for a time when the Messiah would make prophets of all of God's people and fulfill the words of Numbers 25:25.[4]

The Messiah came as the great "prophet" who proclaimed God's Word as the prophets had formerly done, to announce the restoration of God's Kingdom. He acted out prophetically parables and His teachings (e.g Mat. 21:18–22) in the tradition of the earlier prophets like Jeremiah, Ezekiel, and Isaiah.

The Messiah's miracles were like those of the prophet Elijah and Elisha. He understood Himself in the ranks of the prophets.[5] In fact, many recognized Jesus the prophet who was expected (Luke 7:16; Mat. 21:11,46; John 4:19; 6:14; 7:40 9:17). After the resurrection, Peter proclaims Jesus to be a prophet like Moses, the one promised by God in Deuteronomy.[6]

The Holy Spirit or the spirit of prophecy plays an essential role in the divine activity of establishing God's Kingdom in the world. Zechariah reveals this concerning the Spirit of God, "Not by might, nor by power, but my Spirit, says the Lord of Hosts" (4:6). He further states in verse 14 of chapter four a vision of two olive trees that are said to be "the two anointed ones [literally 'sons of oil'] who stand by the Lord of the whole earth." An interesting parallel to all this is Revelation 11:3,10 of the two witnesses who are "the two olive trees and the two lamp stands that stand before the Lord of the earth." John the revealer is showing like Zachariah's vision that these two prophets are anointed with the oil of God's Spirit.

One can see quickly the link between the church's prophetic witness to the world (symbolized by the ministry of the two witnesses) and the universality of this witness with Zechariah's phrase, "stand before the Lord of the earth." It is not the individual's Christian witness to the world that is primary here, but the church's witness to the world which is prophetic (Rev. 11:3–13).[7]

The Holy Spirit inspires prophetic utterance among God's prophets and His church and brings the testimony of Jesus to the whole earth. God therefore brings heavenly revelations to His people (a fulfillment of Acts 2:17) and even directs the prayers of the churches to their heavenly

Lord. Therefore, it is the Spirit of prophecy (the testimony of Jesus) in God's church that brings all nations to worship the one true God.

> *After Moses received the Torah at Sinai and offered it to the people of Israel, he longed to penetrate even deeper into the mystery of the divine so he asked God one day, "O Lord, Sovereign of the Universe, please show me Your ways." Knowing that no man can fathom God's ways and the great danger lies in any attempt to do so, God answered, "You cannot see My face. For you have asked for something you cannot comprehend much less shall perish in doing so. But if you wish, I shall show you My back. Seeing My back, you may perceive what lies behind it, including My own being, the power of My name, and the radiance of My glory." Moses replied, "I beseech thee then to show me Your back." At that moment, God moved past Moses, and as soon as he passed by, he revealed to Moses his awesome back. Suddenly Moses beheld God's glory and light. Time seemed to stand still as liquid flowed from God's presence and he saw a great wind which was the Holy Spirit. Thus it is written, "And the Spirit of God hovered over the waters." Moses saw God's creative life-giving Spirit. Suddenly Moses understood: What transpired at creation transpires all throughout history and time. God's creative power and glory contains the past, the present, and the future. God's back is before us. And on the other side, the side that forever eludes us, is the radiance of His face.*

And now we understand, "God, who at various times and in various ways spoke in times past to the fathers by the prophets, has in these last days spoken to us by His Son, whom He has appointed heir of all things, through whom also He made the world" (Heb. 1:1–2).

❋ The King's Dance

Among the wonders that the Queen of Sheba came to behold in the court of King Solomon was the marvelous throne upon which he sat. It was made of ivory overlaid with the finest gold. Because King Solomon's throne was a seat of judgment, it was surrounded by seventy thousand other thrones, upon which there sat sages, scholars, priests, Levites, and princes of Israel. When the king ascended the steps of his throne, he would bless and praise the Holy Name of the Lord. As the King mounted the steps, the people shouted: "The King shall not multiply wives unto himself" they cried, as he mounted the first step. "The King shall not multiply horses unto himself," they declared at the second. "The King shall not hoard gold and silver to himself," was heard at the third step. "You shall not pervert justice," was the warning uttered at the fourth. "You shall not be partial to anyone," he was told when he came to the fifth. "You shall take no bribes," was the injunction declared at the sixth step. And when he was about to take his seat on the royal throne all cried out, "Know before whom you stand!"

There is no other but the One true God who is the Sovereign King of Kings and Lord of Lords. Israel wanted to be like the other nations and have a human king which God reluctantly granted. God is King over the universe and all other kings receive their authority from him who has all power and authority.

There is a cosmic battle of evil against good where God's rightful Kingdom is embattled against the forces of evil and its dark kingdoms. Rabbinic teaching says that man is free to choose which kingdom he wants to inherit: God's Kingdom of light and love, or Satan's kingdom of darkness and destruction.

One of the greatest battles God's people have concerns their identity and knowing they are God's beloved.[1] Once the Hasidic Rabbi Shelomo was asked, "What is the worst thing the evil urge can achieve?" He answered, "To make man forget that he is a son of a King."

The Messiah literally means "anointed one." The Messiah was not only a prophet but also God's Priest and King. Echoes of Scripture viewed the Messiah as Israel's Savior and King.[2] The Messiah is to usher in God's Kingdom and millennial reign of peace. From the beginning, God intended to have "a kingdom of priests and a holy nation" (Exo. 19:6). Even though many earthly kings were evil and ruled with corruption, the Messiah would rule with righteousness and justice.

The people of Israel have always looked for the coming of the Messiah and the age of His Kingdom. In the new covenant, Yeshua/Jesus has made His followers priests and kings (Rev. 1:6). The Messiah was rejected by His own people just as most nations have often rejected their own prophets and God's messengers. But through the Messiah, there will be a united covenant people of Jews and Gentiles following the Hebrew Bible imagery as "a chosen people, a royal priesthood, a holy nation, a people belonging to God" (1Pe. 2:9).

The Messiah brings the offices of priest, prophet, and king together.[3] Now all followers of the Messiah are to be a kingdom of priests who serve God as they rule on the earth (Rev. 5:10). The power of God raises people to new life, and they will be priests of God and Christ and reign with him for a thousand years (Rev. 20:6). The Lordship of the Lamb will be manifested on earth by the royalty of His people.

Every tribe, tongue, people, and nations falls under the government and Kingship of the Messiah King. Just as the Lamb laid down His life and became the royal Lion King, so Christians lay their lives down for the Messiah which will lead to the conversion of the nations and a righteous remnant of all nations will enter into God's Kingdom.

In the book of Revelation, we get a glimpse of successive visions which get clearer and clearer until the heavenly Jerusalem and sanctuary descends upon earth. God's promise to dwell with His people Israel (Eze. 37:27–28; Zec. 8:8) is manifested by the many nations which will dwell in Zion (Zec. 2:10–11; Isa. 19:25; 56:7; Amo. 9:12). In the New Jerusalem, they will worship God in His immediate presence as priests (Rev. 22:3–4) and as kings (Rev. 22:5).

The extraordinary picture from the book of Revelation is the old creation is filled with God's manifest glory and presence. God's love, forgiveness and reconciliation restores a fallen humanity. When evil is abolished then God's throne comes to earth (Rev. 21:3). After judgment, God Himself Scripture depicts as wiping the tears from the very faces of His people who have suffered so much (21:4). All of Scripture points to the victory of God, the only true and rightful King, and His people who worship and reign with Him.

A king took great delight in music that he appointed the best musicians in his kingdom to play for him each morning. Those who arrived at the designated hour received a handsome reward, and those who came early were rewarded even more handsomely. The musicians, however, were so devoted to the king that they came not for the rewards he bestowed upon them but out of love for the monarch. As the years went by, the musicians passed away one by one. Their sons tried to take their places in service to the king, but they did not have their father's skills, and their instruments were in very poor condition. Worse than their lack of skill and their ill-kept instruments was the fact that they did not have the same love for the king that had animated their fathers. They were interested only in the rewards that the king offered them for showing up at the designated hour. As one might expect, the sound they made was so terrible that the king soon gave up listening to them. Among the sons of the deceased musicians, however, were a few who were concerned not with rewards but with whether or not they were worthy of being the king's servants. Therefore they were determined to learn the art of their fathers and attend to the care of their instruments. Often they would rise in the morning to tune their instruments and practice their music, so that sometimes they would be late in arriving at the court. When they finally entered to the harsh sounds that were coming from the other musicians, they would go off into a corner and play as best as they could. Long after the other musicians had departed they would continue to practice, so that they might better serve the king. The king was well aware of these efforts — nothing escaped his attention — and he was very pleased by them. While they did not play with the same skill as their fathers, their devotion was just as great. And their music filled the king with joy.

The Dance *of* Exile

When the holy city of Jerusalem was under siege at the hands of the Babylonians, the affliction of Israel was terrible indeed. Neighbor turned against neighbor, and most of the prominent men of Israel turned their backs on their brothers. Therefore, the Holy One, blessed be he, turned his face from all of Israel. For as Rabbi Azaryah teaches, when Israel does not abide by the will of the Omnipresent, they weaken, if one may say so, the power of Him who is above all creation. Likewise, when they live by His will, they add strength to the heavenly powers. The sages say: 'God is the shadow of man.' The Temple was made not only of stones but of the will of the Holy One. When we do not follow His will, those who are most holy in our lives — our children — suffer. It is through our children that the heavenly powers manifest themselves. It is thanks to our children that the heavens receive our prayers. How do we follow the will of the Holy One? By attending to our children, whose lives are at stake in our observance of God's Torah. It happened, therefore, that when the soldiers of Babylon came and took away the members of the Sanhedrin, the great court housed in the Temple, the exile of those sages was a terrible blow to all of Israel. No longer did the halls of the Temple echo with the interpretations of the law and commentaries on the Torah. The Shekinah, nonetheless, continued to abide in the Land. Next the Babylonians seized the Temple singers, who ceaselessly uttered God's praise, and sent them into exile. That, too, was a terrible blow to Israel, for the songs sung to God in joy and thanksgiving — the two means of drawing nigh unto the Lord — were heard no more in the Temple. Nevertheless, the Shekinah continued to dwell in the land. Then came the most terrible blow of all, the blow that truly announced the destruction of the truth of the Temple. For next the Babylonians came and took the children into exile. No more were lips unsullied by sin heard to utter words of Torah and offer to God prayers that only they can offer. And so, when the children of Israel were sent into exile, the Shekinah went into exile with them.

The Talmud says:

> *They were exiled to Egypt and the Shekinah was with them; as it is said, 'Did I indeed exile Myself to the house of thy father when they were in Egypt?' (1Sa. 2:27). They were exiled to Babylon and the Shekinah was with them; as it is said, 'For your sake I was sent to Babylon' (Isa. 43:14). Also when in the future they will be redeemed, the Shekinah will be with them; as it is said, 'The Lord will return with thy captivity' (Deu. 30:3). It is not stated, 'The Lord will restore,' but 'will return with' which teaches that the Holy One, blessed be He, will come back with them.[1]*

Spiritually, exile is seen in Israel as a kind of death and a 'return' from exile is a kind of resurrection. Exile is therefore a punishment of Israel for its sin and wickedness as well as a sacrifice of redemptive suffering. Just as God is reforming and restoring all creation, God is forming and restoring His people Israel.

In one sense, Israel is still in exile until the full restoration of Temple and return of the Messiah happens. Even during the time of Jesus, Jews still had a sense of exile under pagan oppressors (Rome) and the time of Judgment is prayed to cease so that God's restoration would come and God finally vindicates His people at last.

The story of Israel is thus a story of God's restoration of all of creation. Israel's story subverts and confronts all other stories as the clash between good and evil, exile and restoration, fall and recreation all come together in Israel's history and narrative. Jewish kingdom language by the Messiah also expresses the hope and vision of Israel's restoration, the rebuilding of the Temple, and the return of *YHVH* to Zion.

All messianic people look forward to the age of vindication and the victory of God. *YHVH* would finally be king and do for Israel what the prophets had foretold a long time ago. Therefore exile and restoration are two central tenets of Israel's story being enacted out in human history. The Messiah tells a story about a prodigal coming back to Father God. This parable is a call to Israel and all Jews to return to the Father, as Jeremiah had spoken of (Jer. 31:18–20).

The story has deepened but its still the story of Israel coming to terms with their covenant-making God. The long awaited Messiah had finally come in *Yeshua*/Jesus and those who oppose him end up rejecting God's Son in human form. The one true God of the Shema through election and covenant revealed Himself in the one who Israel's hopes and vision of the end centered which is none other than the Messiah Himself.

The Jesus story then is not a new religion to replace an old out-dated one but a new act in God's redemptive history within the continuous story of Israel. Christians are not to abandon the classic Jewish story but to understand it as a long awaited new phase and moment in the same story. This renewed story of God establishing His Kingdom on earth has changed the destinies of men and women who give their allegiance foremost to God and not to the empire and world domination system.

The Messiah's subversive parables retold the story of Israel in such a way that He invited them into a new way of being Israel. There was a sense of urgency and immediacy to Jesus' words. There was a revealing and concealing with challenges like "If you have ears, then hear!" Even the Messianic secret could not be kept secret for very long.[2]

God has sent a retrieval or rescue mission to His people and for all the nations and it has come by sending His Son who sets the captives free which is none other than the Messiah who delivers His people out of exile into God's restoration hope and future. God's messianic plan brings forth judgment and mercy, hardening and deliverance, retrieval and renewal. The return of the king YHVH will bring defeat to evil and He will judge those who resist His rule.

The Messiah's words are sharpest especially to His own people. Israel and all who follow God are spoken to in the severest prophetic terms. There is the dual message to Israel of open warm welcomes and severe stern warnings. The Messiah fulfilled all of Israel's prophecies and calls her people and all nations to return from exile.

The Sabbath Dance

Among the Jews, the observance of the Sabbath, the day of the Lord, was origi-
nally a thing of joy. But too many Rabbis kept issuing one injunction after an-
other until some people felt they could hardly move during the Sabbath for fear
that some regulation or other might be transgressed. The Baal Shem, son of Eli-
ezer, gave much thought to this matter. One night he had a dream. An angel
took him up to heaven and showed him two thrones placed far above all others.
In his dream Baal Shem visited a man who was to be his companion in paradise.
He found him living among the Gentiles quite ignorant of Jewish customs; and,
on the Sabbath, he would give a banquet at which there was a lot of merrymak-
ing, and to which all his Gentle neighbors were invited. When Ball Shem asked
him why he held the banquet, the man replied, "I recall that in my childhood my
parents taught me that the Sabbath was a day of rest and for rejoicing; so on
Saturdays my Mother made the most succulent meals at which we sang and
danced and made merry. I do the same today." Baal Shem attempted to instruct
the man in the ways of religion, for he had been born a Jew but was evidently
quite ignorant of all the rabbinical prescriptions. But Baal Shem was struck
dumb when he realized that the man's joy in the Sabbath would be marred if he
was made aware of this shortcoming. Baal Shem, still in his dream, then went to
the home of his companion in hell. He found the man to be a strict observer of
the Law, always apprehensive lest his conduct should not be correct. The poor
man spent each Sabbath day in scrupulous tension as if he were sitting on hot
coals. When Baal Shem attempted to upbraid him for his slavery to the Law, the
power of speech was taken away from him as he realized that the man would
never understand that he could do wrong by fulfilling religious injunctions.
Thanks to this revelation given him in the form of a dream, Baal Shem evolved a
new system of observance whereby God is worshipped in joy that comes from the
heart.

The Sabbath is the seventh day of the week, Saturday, whereas most Christians celebrate it on the first day, Sunday. It is a day set aside from the other six as a day which God blessed and made holy "because on it God rested from all His work which He had done in creation" (Gen. 2:3). The Talmud says that "the Sabbath is to be a day of light and beauty and Godliness."[1] The Sabbath is a holy day for a holy people.

The Sabbath is also a day to do good rather than to be some kind of binding rule that keeps people from loving their neighbors. For example, one obligation prescribed by the Talmud: "To the vagrant beggar must be given no less than a loaf worth of bread and flour. If he stays overnight, he is to be provided with sleeping accommodations; and if he stays over the Sabbath, he must receive food for three meals."[2]

"Six days a week we wrestle with the world, wringing profit from the earth; on the Sabbath we especially care for the seed of eternity planted in the soul… Six days a week we dominate the world, on the seventh day we try to dominate the self."[3] The world is filled with so much noise and flurry that it needs the seeds of eternity to bring it rest. The Sabbath is God's way of telling us to "Stop!" or "Quit it!" This Hebrew word rings a melody of wonder and astonishment in taking notice of God's work while one rests from one's own labor.

When all of God's work was done at creation, God rested. All of our work is done now in the context of God's work. Sabbath-keeping is not just about one day a week being holy but every day being holy for the Lord.[4] Sabbath-keeping aligns our lives with the very rhythms of creation itself. The danger is when people distort the Sabbath and turn it into something it was never meant to be in the first place. Even Yeshua/Jesus exposed the dangers of legalism and bondage to the Sabbath and restored it to the precious gift it actually is from God (see Mark 2:23–28; 3:1–6; Luke 14:1–6; John 5:1–18; 9:1–41).

The seasons of life also mark seasons of worship, resting, listening, and blessing. Can we discern the times and moments where God's beauty, revelation, presence, and glory burst forth on the scene? Or do we become slaves to the machine of work where work empties any sense of the presence of God in our lives? Sabbath-wonder should be a part of our everyday lives and scheduled activities. Finding our own rhythms and cycles of rest, adventure, creation exploring, and worship expanding horizons.

The Sabbath when followed brings balance, adoration, humble acknowledgment that we are not masters of the world around us, but that there is only one master and King of the universe — God. Humility and joy springs from it that shouts "enter, O Bride, enter, O Bride!"[5] Love fulfills it! One of the prayers that the Rabbis recite is:

From Thy love, O Lord, O Lord our God, wherewith thou didst love Thy people Israel, and from the compassion, which thou didst feel for the children of Thy covenant, Thou didst give us, O Lord our God, this great and holy seventh day in love.[6]

It is through and in the Sabbath that we discover God's best for us is in the work He has done for us. All the barriers of work and rest, discipline and joy, silence and attentive wonder to God's ways cross together in the Messiah's love for He taught us to love God foremost and to love one another (Deu. 6:5; Mat. 22:37–39).

Rabbi Yeshaiah had an argument with God. It seemed, week after week, God failed to provide him with the things that he needed for the observance of the Sabbath until the last minute. Wednesday and Thursday and most of Friday would go by before he would have the things required in order to properly keep the Sabbath. His question was "Why?" He was a poor Rabbi and he would spend most of the week worrying about where and how he would be able to aquire the things he needed for observing the Sabbath. He would spend hours in a state of anxiety. Greatly distressed over all this, Rabbi Yeshaiah took his case to God and argued, "Master of the Universe! Since You somehow never fail to provide me with the things I need to keep your holy Sabbath, I have one small request to make of you. I beg You, O Lord, could You please provide me the things I need on Wednesday or Thursday, instead of making me worry until late on Friday where many of the Merchants take advantage financially of my wife because we are purchasing the things we need so late in the week for the Sabbath. If you could provide for me earlier in the week, I could do much more with much less. Then I would have all the provisions for the Sabbath, and my soul would be free of its anguish and longing."The Holy One, replied to the Rabbi, "You need not concern yourself, my son, with what these provisions may cost on Friday late afternoon. For I have the silver, and I have the gold. As for the longing in your soul, which arises from a love for My Holy Day, that is precisely what I want from you."

❀ | *The* Dance *of* Compassion

There were two brothers who shared a farm. They each had their own livestock and granary, and they split the profits evenly. However, one of the brothers married and had a large family. The other brother was single. One day the single brother thought, "it is not fair that I receive half of the farm's profits when my brother is married and has children to care for. Why should I receive half when my brother has a greater need?" That night he prepared a large sack of grain, carried it to the door of his brother's barn, and placed it there. Now the next morning, the married brother went to his barn and was startled to see that he had the extra sack of grain. He thought, "It is not fair that my brother and I divide the profits of the farm evenly. After all, I have a wife and children to care for me in my old age. My brother is alone in this world. He can use this grain more than I can." That night, the married brother carried the sack of grain to his brother's barn and placed it at the door. This went on for several days, with each of the brothers carrying a sack of grain to the other's barn. One night, the two brothers met each other on the way, each carrying a sack of grain. They dropped the sacks, ran toward each other and embraced, understanding at last the love they had for one another.

God is the pattern for human life and Scripture repeatedly says things like "walk in all His ways" (Deu. 11:22) and "the Lord God is full of compassion and gracious, slow to anger, and abounding in mercy and truth" (Exo. 34:6). God is continually described as compassionate and gracious, and so we are to be people full of compassion and grace. The golden rule and loving thy neighbor as yourself are foundational in rabbinic thought. All believers are to imitate God and to show kindness and compassion toward others because we all come from a common ancestry and every person is created in the divine likeness of God.[1]

Jewish thought teaches that kindly deeds helps alleviate burdens and sweetens human relationships. One of the central tenets of following God as a way of life comes from Mic. 4:8, "To do justly, to love mercy, and to walk humbly." All of life is a living sacrifice of love to God and neighbor. The Talmud says, "He that is gracious to the poor lendeth unto the Lord" and "He that is gracious unto the needy honoureth Him."[2] There is no aspect of life that does not come under the divine governance of God.

There is much rabbinic teaching concerning living as resident aliens and this earthly life is not all there is or our home. The story of exile and being a guest is part and parcel of Israel's story. For example, a story of Hillel says, "When he ended his lesson with his disciples, he accompanied them part of the way. They asked him, 'Master, where are you going?' 'To bestow an act of kindness upon a guest who is in my house... have you, then, a guest always with you?'"[3] Jewish hospitality and generosity were not just ideals for Jewish community but the heart and soul of it.

At the center of the covenant is mutual love and compassion even for outsiders. The compassion of God so fills His people that the sick are helped, the grieving comforted, and the hungry fed. Doing these good deeds in Jewish teaching does not earn God's love or approval but comes through the grace and love of God that empowers people to serve and be a blessing to others.

Jewish hospitality starts with the family but extends to all kinds of occasions and circumstances. The Rabbis teach that showing hospitality produces the works of God. Or "He who greets the learned is as if he greeted God."[4] Those who gave alms and aid to the poor fulfills the Torah and reveals God's stamp on one's life. God's righteousness is none other that the divine light and *shekinah* flowing through His people to family, friends, and outsiders.

Compassion and charity mark and distinguish the people of God. The Talmud says, "Great is charity, for it brings the redemption of the Messiah near."[5] The character of God's compassion and generosity is a description for the very character of God's people. The Messiah would not only bring peace but would reflect the divine character and glory of God. It's interesting to note that Jesus encounter's with large numbers of people (the crowds) to particular people who needed healing was motivated by the heart of God that is described as compassion.[6] Even when the wicked deserved punishment and Jesus disciples asked him to call fire down from heaven to destroy them, Jesus resisted because of the grace of God and divine compassion (Luke 9:51–56).

A Torah based life is a life of showing lovingkindness and compassion. Torah never stands alone as a book to be read but also to be obeyed and lived. Love for God and man is central to the way of life people are to follow. All of Jewish wisdom is drawn deep from the wells of God's compassion and love. Nothing is complete or done well without these essential marks. Rabbi Paul says it like this:

> If I give all I posses to the poor and surrender my body to the flames but have not love, I gain nothing. Love is patient, love is kind. It does not envy, it does not boast, it is not proud. It is not rude, it is not self-seeking, it is not easily angered, it keeps no record of wrongs. Love does not delight in evil but rejoices with the truth. It always protects, always trusts, always hopes, always perseveres. Love never fails... And now these three remain: faith, hope and love. But the greatest of these is love (1Cor. 13:3–8a,13).

I love the rabbinic tale that tells of a righteous man who was allowed to see heaven and hell:

> First he was ushered to hell, where he saw people seated at a most alluring banquet table. The people seated at the table appeared to be emaciated and frail, as if they had not eaten for weeks. Near each of them, however, were heaping plates of food. "Why don't the people partake of the food?" the man asked his guide. "Ah, well," said the guide, "as you can see, each person at the table had arms that cannot bend. They are unable to feed themselves." "Truly this is hell," said the man. Later, the man was ushered to heaven, where he beheld much of the same scene: a large festive table laden with food, and people whose arms could not bend. These people, however, were not starving and weak, but happy and well fed. "I don't understand," said the man. "Heaven appears to be no different than hell." "Yes," said the guide, "but with one noticeable exception. Here the people are happy and well fed. In hell they think only of feeding themselves. In heaven they have learned to feed each other."

❀ | *The* Dance *of* Fasting

The Jews of Sasov were gathered in the synagogue one Yom Kippur eve to hear Rabbi Moshe-Leib chant the Kol Nidre, the most important prayer of the year. Then, as now, people who never regularly attended synagogue at any other time were on hand for this prayer, and they eagerly awaited the appearance of the rabbi. But, strange to say, as the moment for the recitation of the prayer approached, Rabbi Moshe Leib had not shown up."Where could he be?' the congregates asked one another, growing more worried with each passing second. After all, Moshe Leib was known for being in the right place at the right time, for joining words with meaning at precisely the moment when words were called for. It was unthinkable that he should fail to be present for the Kol Nidre. They began to fear that something terrible had happened to him. Indeed, some wondered whether they should go look for the rabbi, but no one was sure where to look. If he was not in the synagogue, with all the Jews of Sasov, where could he possibly be? Among those who sat and waited for the rabbi was a young widow who lived near the synagogue. That evening she left her infant son at home, sleeping in his cradle, just long enough to come and hear the chanting of Kol Nidre. Surely, she said to herself, it will not take too long for just this one prayer, the most important of all prayers. Five minutes went by and then ten, minutes that seemed like an eternity. Finally, the mother felt that she could wait no longer and hurried home to her little one. When she walked into her house, whom should she behold but Rabbi Moshe Leib sitting in a rocking chair and singing a lullaby to the babe. Somewhat apologetically, the rabbi looked up at the surprised woman and explained, "I was on my way to the synagogue for the Kol Nidre service. As I was passing by your house, I heard your child crying. What else could I do but come in and comfort the baby?" What is even more important than fasting and praying the Kol Nidre? Rabbi Moshe Leib knew: more important than fasting and giving the most important prayer is the comfort given to a child in distress.

Fasting is a way to cleanse one's body, physically and spiritually.[1] Fasting prepares one to hear from God and to seek after God with all one's heart and focus. Isaiah 58:6–8 says:

> *Is not this the fast I have chosen? To loose the bands of wickedness, to undo the heavy burdens, and to let the oppressed go free, and that ye break every yoke? Is it not to deal thy bread to the hungry, and that thou bring the poor that are cast out of thy house? when thou seest the naked, that thou cover; and that thou hide not thyself from thine own flesh? Then shall thy light breakforth as the morning, and thine health shall spring forth speedily: and thy righteousness shall go before thee; the glory of the Lord shall be thy reward.*

Fasting and prayer brings forth the power and glory of God! Joel says it simply like this, "Turn to Me with all you heart, with fasting" (2:12). Fasting frees us from the addictions of sin.[2] It helps solves life problems we face and gives us a divine perspective when we seek the face and will of God. Fasting turns our concerns and burdens over to the Lord. It liberates the poor and sets the captive free. Fasting brings healing and protection from the evil one.[3]

Fasting is ultimately an act of self-denial.[4] We see in Scripture fasting as a normal expression of grief and a way of showing one's remorse of sin. David said, "I humbled myself with fasting" (Psa. 35:13). Humility and self-surrender removes self so God can do His work in us. Scripture even recognizes corporate sins that need to be confessed corporately through prayer and fasting (Dan. 9; Ezr. 8).

We see throughout biblical Israel times of national mourning and fasting (1Ki. 21:27; Jon. 3:3–4) when faced with God's judgment as well as grave danger (2Ch. 20:2–3; Est. 4:15–16). Israel fasted while reading Scripture (Neh. 9:1–3; Jer. 36:10) and fasted at times of joy and great gladness (Zec. 8:19).

The great "Day of Atonement" of prayer and fasting is *Yom Kippur* described in Leviticus 23:27, "Also the tenth day of the seventh month shall be the Day of Atonement. It shall be a holy convocation for you; you shall afflict your souls, and offer and offering made by fire to the Lord." Even the latter testament describes Christians and Jews fasting during the time of *Yom Kippur* (Acts 27:9).

The Messiah fasted and expected people to pray and fast (Mat. 4:1 –2; 6:2,5,16). Christian teachers and prophets fasted in Antioch (Acts 13:2) and Paul was "in fastings often" (2Cor. 11:27). The apostles tried unsuccessfully to exorcise a demonized boy; Jesus taught them that "this kind goeth not out but by prayer and fasting" (Mat. 17:21). One of the ways the power of heaven and the Kingdom of God invades earth is through the spiritual discipline of fasting.

Not only do prayer and fasting go together, but fasting for break-through is similar to prayer. Just as prayer can be a continuous process of faith and waiting for God's response, so fasting builds our faith and character as one continually focuses on God. The longer we fast, the longer we walk in faith and obedience. The longer we abstain from food, the more determined our faith becomes. After a time, our faith grows and our trust increases as the spirit world more and more impacts our soul.

Scripture tells us to lean not on our own understanding and to trust God by obeying His Word and listening to His Spirit when it comes to times and seasons of fasting. In Matthew 6, the Messiah teaches the secrecy of fasting. He is not saying its wrong to let others know you are fasting but rather, avoid acting superior or boasting to others about your fasting.

Fasting is done with both humility and faith determination. Its not about exalting ourselves but exalting God and giving Him the glory in everything one does.[5] There is also power in fasting done corporately with other Christians. Fasting breaks the bondage of the flesh over our will and frees our spirits to soar with God who is sovereign over every circumstance and situation we face. From Moses to the Messiah, fasting prepares one to hear and obey God who brings abundant life for all who seek Him.

❈ | *The* Dance *of* Offering

There once lived a man who built a house overlooking a village. Now this man was compassionate and generous, and he always helped his neighbors whenever he could. As was his habit, he would stand at a large window each morning and look down on the village, count his blessings, and say a prayer for his friends. Each day he would do at least one good deed, and would return to his home joyous and content. Now it came to pass that the man gained a sizable sum of money. He thanked God for this good fortune and resolved to help others with his money. He did, however, make one concession for himself. He decided to adorn the edges of his favorite window with pure silver. As the days went by, the man gave to his neighbors. He began every morning by standing at the window giving thanks for his blessings. But he also wondered how much more beautiful the window might be if it had additional silver around the edges. Days went by, then weeks, then months. As time passed, the fellow gave less of his time and money to those in need and spent more of his wealth on adorning the window. Eventually the entire glass was covered with glowing silver. In the end, the fellow could no longer see his neighbors from the window. He could only see his own reflection.

Money is not a possession to be hoarded, but something to be shared. If money became an idol, then one should dispossess oneself of it.[1] Deceitful wealth chokes the Torah out of people. Money is a gift which is to aid the poor and be a blessing to others.

The Talmud says, "What should a man do to secure sons? Let him spend his money freely on the poor."[2] The blessing of God is on those who show charity and generosity to the needy. Just as God has showered man with grace, so should man be gracious to others. To lend to the poor is like lending to the Lord.

The Jewish people gave tithes, offerings, and even paid a temple tax. Leviticus 27:30–33 mandates a tenth of all the produce goes to the Lord. Numbers 18:8–32 explains that these tithes and offerings were to be given to the Levites, who in turn would tithe to the priests (18:21). Every third year, tithes would go to local storehouses so that they could also be distributed among the poor, "the aliens, the fatherless, and widows" (Deu. 14:29).

Ancient Israel had forced labor under the Monarchy and paid many tributes and taxes. They gave to the royal tax and emergency tribute during wartime They also had to pay the temple tax and leave the gleanings of their fields open during sabbatical and jubilee years. All the while they were to give of their firstfruits and other voluntary offerings along with their "triple tithe."[3]

Numerous texts from the Hebrew Bible call for God's people a "redeemed economics" of sharing with the poor and administrating justice and fairness not only among their own people but even to the surrounding nations. God recognizes man's helplessness and His people are to see it as well.

There was a kind of "sliding scale" when it came to the offerings and sacrifices to God (see Lev. 5:7,11; 12:8; 14:21–22). If the poor could not afford to sacrifice their livestock, there were provisions for them to replace them with doves and young pigeons. Even flour could be a substitute for the poorest of the poor.

There were also provisions in the law where partiality was forbidden and justice must be equitable. Some compliances for the poor included penalties of theft (Exo. 22:2), the payment of a vow (Lev. 27:8) and the celebration of Passover (Exo. 12:4).[4]

The greatest offering a person could give in rabbinic wisdom literature was to offer oneself to the Lord. Sacrifices from the abundance of what one has was good but nothing exceeded the gift of offering oneself completely and unreservedly to God.[5]

There are many parallels between generous giving in both testaments of the Bible which prescribes not to boast in riches but to be generous in giving them away (Jer. 9:23–24; see 1Cor. 1:26–29). God gives kindness, justice, and righteousness to the earth and so should God's people economics and politics be governed by these same principles.

Malachi 3:8–10 describes how Israel is robbing God of her tithes and offerings. Malachi 3:10 says, "Bring the whole tithe into the storehouse, that there may be food in my house." This call to faithful obedience in giving the full amount God is unique to the covenant with Israel, whereas application in the New Testament era may take some different shape and forms.[6]

The material blessings God gave to Israel confirmed His blessing and promise to build a mighty nation out of them. Israel was to share their covenantal blessings and Torah with the whole world. This principle of generosity and compassion with one's material blessings is for Israel and the church to recognize God's ownership of the world and to share their blessings with all the nations.

The age of the Messiah would be a time of prosperity and abundant blessings. The Messiah would put all things under His feet, even the frantic concern for economic survival. For the Messiah would reveal true riches are not found in the deceitfulness of greed and wealth but real discipleship is in giving generously to those in need (Luke 10)

There is both a blessing of giving and receiving. In our culture today, it may even be easier to give than for some people to receive, but it is in receiving that all parties are blessed by God. God's covenant faithfulness is the wellspring for being rich towards God in faith and good deeds to others.

> While some rabbis were dining, a holy man, very old, got up and attempted to serve the rabbis. But no one would take so much as a cup of water from the old man except Rabbi Abraham. The others were shocked about this and later said to him, "How is it that you considered yourself worthy to accept the service of that holy man?" Rabbi Abraham replied, "Well, when I offer people a drink of water, I'm happy if they take it. Did you expect me to sadden the old man by depriving him of the joy of giving me something?"

The Victory *of* God

❀ | *The* Victory *of* Prayer

As Ari stood in the synagogue praying, and angel appeared at his side. Ari did not notice the angel until the angel whispered in his ear. "You think you know how to pray?" the angel asked. "I know of a man whose prayers have penetrated the highest reaches of Heaven. His name is Amos, and he lives in Tiberias. If you want to know what prayers are most precious to the Holy One, you must seek him out." Ari lost no time heeding the angels words. He immediately set off for Tiberias to seek out the man whose prayers were so precious to God. Ari searched the house of study but he was not there. He searched the marketplace but he was not there either. But one man told him of a poor farmer who lived in the mountains on the outskirts of the city. "Could it be," he asked himself, "that a simple farmer has mastered what masters themselves cannot?" Ari went up the mountain and came to a modest hut. He knocked and a man answered. Ari inquired, "Are you the one called Amos?" "I am," the man replied. "Please come in." Happy to have found the man, he wasted no time and said, "Please, I have come to learn from you the secret of your prayers." Puzzled and somewhat embarrassed by Ari's request, the man replied, "But Rabbi, I do not know how to pray. I cannot even read, and so the prayer book is closed to me. All I know is how to recite a few letters of the alphabet, from alef to yud." Ari could not believe his ears. Had the angel not declared to him that the prayers of this man were precious in God's sight? "Were you in prayer just recently" Ari asked. "Yes," he replied. "When I heard in the synagogue how beautiful and passionate everyone else around me was praying, my heart overflowed with longing. Suddenly, as though they had a life of their own, the letters of the alphabet came to my lips. In the depths of my heart I said, "Dear God, Lord of the Universe, please take these letters from my lips and make them into prayers that will rise up into Your ears, as it pleases You, my Lord!" That is the prayer I repeat over and over, a prayer about praying." After hearing this, Ari realized that God blessed this humble man and had revealed to him the secret of the prayer most precious to the Holy One: It is the prayer that rises up from the heart — the true dwelling place of Him who dwells in the highest reaches of heaven.

The Rabbis teach that prayer is greater than sacrifices and good deeds.[1] True prayer is more than the utterance of the lips but must come from the depths of the heart. It is prayer for the voice for mercy, a cry for justice, a plea for humility. Prayer is the place where heaven and earth meet.

Rabbinic thought teaches that prayer is not to impose man's will upon God, but to allow God to impose His will and mercy upon the one praying. Prayer is the home of the soul. Jews rightly combine Scripture and prayer together in forming prayers that cannot be prayed without God's help. A prayer from the Talmud goes, "I give thanks before Thee, O Lord my God, that Thou has set my portion with those who sit in the House of Study and not with those who sit at street corners."[2]

In prayer man comes trembling to God and finds sanctuary for the soul. God draws close in prayer and brings everything more into focus in a world that is often coming unraveled. The great exchange happens in prayer from our will to God's wisdom. Even in the inexpressible, sighs too deep for words, God gives peace and strength and a daring confidence (to even do the impossible for Him).

Rabbinical tradition has an idea they call *kavvanah*, where a person is so touched by God that not only are the person's words a prayer, but the person "becomes" the prayer. One would so meditate on the law of God that one could say it over and over again (*hagah*).

Families in the Jewish tradition came together and the children would learn to chant and sing the scriptures "out loud" until it was known by heart. This is why every syllable of the Hebrew Scriptures was accompanied by a set of musical notations called "tropes."[3] The whole Old Testament could be chanted in a sing-song fashion. One could say it was like a kind of ancient Hebrew rap.

Families meditated, studied, and memorized the Word of God together through oral recitation and praying the Bible out loud to God. The whole body was even involved in swaying back and forth in rhythmic meditation on God's Word. Praying with the whole body begins in the flesh but ends up in praying by the Spirit.

It is amazing as one aligns earthly worship with heavenly worship as portrayed in the book of Revelation that all of heaven in unity and rhythmic harmony are praying together out loud.[4] One sees in these heavenly pictures of beings shouting or singing in a loud voice (Rev. 5:12; 6:10).

Passion is at the root of Jewish worship as well as how Jesus prays and worships are the descriptions throughout the Newer Testament of true worship of God. I have just recently began singing my prayers out loud to God, chanting the Scriptures out loud, as well as prayer walking throughout my city with others.

This kind of praying out loud I find is a pathway to the heart of God that enlarges my own small heart. Praying passionately fuels a burning heart that leads to more revelation, hearing God's voice, and revival of one's soul and worship in community.

It is the poverty of spirit and prayer, the divine prompting and urgings from God's Spirit that bring restoration, healing, and God's shekinah glory among God's united people. Prayer then is not something one adds to their life, but is a way of life. Prayer is the place where not only heaven and earth intersect, but where Jews and Gentiles can discover their common destiny together in the plan of God.

When Rabbi Moshe passed away, Rabbi Kotzker asked one of his disciples, "What was the most important thing you remember your teacher taught you?" The student replied, "That is simple, the most important thing he taught us was whatever one happens to be doing at the moment. His every movement was a form of prayer. Therefore, he was present, heart and soul, in his every action. I have never known anyone who was so fully present, before God and man alike, in everything he did."Hearing these words, the Rabbi realized the truth of one of his own sayings. God enters where He is allowed to enter. And He can enter anywhere at any time. But it is our presence in our words and deeds that opens the door for him.

❈ | *The* Victory *of* Angels

Once there was a rich man who wanted to have a banquet. He invited all his friends, especially those of high standing, and purchased the finest foods and the most exotic drinks. On the night before the festivities, he dreamed that his moment of redemption would come during the banquet, and so he was anxious to be on his guard, lest he miss the moment when God would draw near to him. The next evening, during the banquet, he made every effort to talk with each guest, to make certain that everyone was enjoying the festivities. Late in the evening, as the banquet was drawing to a close, one of the host's best friends came to the party with a young boy and girl. The two young people spent the evening dancing together and talking to the other guests. Now the host was first amused by these two, but he grew weary of their youthful zest and energy. Before the party came to a close, the young man and woman approached the host and announced that they would like to be married. The host turned them away, insisting that they were not right for each other, and that they were too young to marry. Furthermore, he asked them to leave the banquet. That night, the rich man had another dream. God told him, "If you had only approved the marriage of the young man and woman your redemption would have come. I was the One who sent them to you. The boy and girl were none other than the angels Michael and Gabriel."

Rabbinic literature describes angels surrounding the throne of God.[1] They are created beings whose purpose is to glorify God. Angels are immortal and therefore do not reproduce their species. Nor are angels subject to normal human passions.[2] The Talmud says that when God created man, "Man resembles the creatures above and the creatures below. Like the animals he eats and drinks, propagates his species, relieves himself and dies. Like the ministering angels he stands erect, speaks, possesses intellect, and sees."[3]

Angels are not intermediaries between God and the world but ministering servants. There are different ranks in the angelic host, like archangels as well as Seraphim, and special duties of angels, like aiding others in worship and prayer.[4] The Talmud says, "After all the places of worship have completed their services, the angel who is appointed over prayer gathers up all the devotions which have been offered in all the places of worship, forms them into crowns and sets them upon the head of the Holy One, blessed is He."[5]

In Scripture, we do not find any angels named until the book of Daniel, where we read about the angels Michael and Gabriel. Michael is described as "one of the chief princes" (10:13) and Gabriel is mentioned in 8:16 as well as 9:21. The Talmud says there are four angels that surround the throne of God. "Michael is on the right, corresponding to the tribe of Reuben; Uriel on its left, corresponding to the tribe of Dan, which was located in the north; Gabriel in front, corresponding to the tribe of Judah as well as Moses and Aaron who were in the east; and Raphael in the rear, corresponding to the tribe of Ephraim which was in the west."[6]

What we see in Torah is each nation has their own guardian angel and Michael being the guardian angel of Israel. The archangel Michael brought news to Sarah that she would give birth to a son, and Michael was the one who instructed Moses while he also protected the Israelites. Michael smote the army of Sennacherib (Exo. 18:5) and when Haman plotted to destroy the Jews in Persia, Michael defended them in heaven.[7]

Gabriel was a messenger of God on many occasions. He was one of the three angels who visited Abraham and his task being to overthrow Sodom. Gabriel was the angel who spoke to Ezekiel in 9:3*ff*. Gabriel also secured the salvation of Israel by preventing Vashti from obeying the King's command and thus securing Esther as queen in her place. Raphael is the prince of healing and Uriel means "light of God" and aids men in their knowledge of God. Dumah is the angel of death. Just as there are righteous angels, so there are wicked angels.

Rabbinic literature is filled with stories of demons and Satan, who is the personification of evil. A rabbinic prayer of blessing says, "May he prosper in all his possessions; may not Satan have power over the works of his hands nor over ours; and may there not leap before him or us any thought of sin, transgression or iniquity from now and for evermore."[8]

The Talmud describes three functions of Satan. "He seduces men; he accuses them before God; he inflicts the punishment of death."[9] Satan is the great deceiver and is always planting doubts, the author of confusion, and brings self-condemnation to men. But Satan is powerless when it comes to the Day of Atonement for Israel. The Talmud says,

"The sounding of the ram's horn (*shofar*) on the new year confounds Satan."[10]

It is interesting in the Apocalyptic tradition that angels refuse to be worshiped.[11] Although the Jewish monotheism of Israel prohibits the worship of angels, we do find the worship of Jesus.[12] John, in his Revelation, portrays the worship of Jesus in chapter 5. An angel says, "Who is worthy?" (5:2) and the rabbinic Jewish picture of a heavenly council proclaims that only the Lamb is worthy, no one else. The angels implement God's divine purpose for history, while the unique role of the Messiah receives worship from a heavenly host (5:8–12).

Throughout all of Scripture there is an angelic liturgy that leads to a face-to-face encounter with God. It may even be possible that by showing hospitality to strangers, some people have entertained angels without knowing it (Heb. 13:2).

There was a child listening attentively to the Rabbi tell the story of the sacrifice of Isaac on the way to Mt. Moriah with his father. Here is what he experienced as he heard the story. "He lay on the alter, bound, waiting to be sacrificed. My heart began to beat faster; it actually sobbed with pity for Isaac. Behold, Abraham now lifted the knife. And now my heart froze within me with fright. Suddenly, the voice of an angel was heard; 'Abraham, lay not your hand upon the lad, for now I know that you fear God.' And here I broke into tears and wept aloud. "Why are you crying?" asked the Rabbi. "You know that Isaac was not killed." And I said to him, still weeping, "But Rabbi, supposing the angel had come too late?" The Rabbi comforted me by telling me that an angel cannot come late.

✿ | *The* Victory *of* Worship

Terach the father of Abram business was selling idols. Abram worked at his father's side in the idol shop. From time to time Abram's father would leave the shop in his son's care. One day a man came into the store to purchase one of the graven images. As Abram watched the customer gaze adoringly upon an idol, Abram was struck with an idea — or a question. "Excuse me, sir," Abram said to the man, "but how old are you, if I may ask?" "Why I am fifty years old," the gentleman replied, puzzled by the lad's question. "Then how is it, sir," asked Abram, "that one who is fifty years old can bring himself to worship an object no older than a day?" The man grew ashamed at the thought and did not know how to answer. Without saying a word he put the idol back he held in his hands and hurried out the store. Abram said nothing to his father about the incident, but he was haunted by his own question and by the man's embarrassment. Soon Abram's bewilderment turned into understanding, and Abram knew he must somehow act on his realization. The next time he was left alone in the shop, a woman came into he store carrying a bowl of flour. "Please," she said, gesturing to the idols that filled the shop, "I'm in a rush. So would you take this flour and offer it to them?" She handed Abram the flour and went on her way. "Yes," the thought occurred to the lad as he gazed at the bowl of flour. "I have just the offering for them." At that Abram took a stick and smashed all the idols but one, the largest one. Then he placed the stick in the hands of the remaining idol and waited until his father's return. He did not have long to wait. When Terach entered the shop, he was horrified at the sight of the broken idols that littered the floor. "What have you done?" he shouted at his son. "Have you lost your mind?" "I cannot hide the truth from you, father," Abram answered. "While you were out a woman came in with a bowl of flour. She asked that I offer it to the idols and then left. I was about to make the offering, when one idol exclaimed, 'Let me be the first to eat!' hearing this, another insisted, 'No, I must be

the first! Just when it looked as though all of them would break out in an argu-
ment, the largest idol rose up, took a stick, and broke the rest. Then he took the
flour for himself." "Are you mocking me, boy?" his father cried. "Do you take me
for a fool? They have no speech or understanding!" "Father, please," Abram
replied, "let your ears hear what your mouth is saying. The true God, the living
God, the Creator of Heaven and earth, is invisible, eternal, and above all flesh. It
is He alone whom we should worship."

God gave His Law to the people as both Israel's Creator and Deliver; the
people's response to God was reverent worship. Israel was called out of
Egypt to sacrifice and worship God (see parallels: Exo. 3:18; 5:1,3; 7:16;
8:1 with Heb. 7:26; Exo. 8:8 with Heb. 8:16; Exo. 8:27 with Heb. 8:23; Exo.
9:1,13; 10:3,7,25–26). All of life is one of ascribing glory to God and serving Him.[1]

To worship God means to bow low and prostrate oneself before
Almighty God. The Hebrew Bible is filled with many examples of this:

- Abraham worshipped God as he went to sacrifice his one and
  only son (Gen. 22:5).
- Eliezer worshipped God for prospering his journey through
  miraculous direction (Gen. 24:26,48,52).
- Moses worshipped on Sinai as God revealed Himself and pro-
  claimed His ways to him (Exo. 34:8–9).
- Joshua worshipped God when he met the Captain of the Lord
  of Hosts (Jos. 5:14).
- Gideon worshipped God gratefully for confirming His will
  (Jdg. 7:13–15).
- Hannah and Elkanah worshipped God for promising them a
  child (1Sa. 1:19).
- Job worshipped God after he had lost everything (Job 1:20–21).
- Jehoshaphat and all the people, reacting to the prophetic word,
  "fell before the Lord, worshiping the Lord" (2Ch. 20:18).
- All the people worshiped during the time of Hezekiah's revival
  (2Ch. 29:28–30).
- The people responded to Ezra's leadership by crying, "Amen,
  Amen, with lifted up hands; and they bowed their heads and
  worshiped the Lord with their faces to the ground" (Neh. 8:6).
  Also amazing is that the people confessed and worshiped for
  a fourth part of a day (9:3).[2]

There are many passages which speak of trained musicians and the glory
of the Lord filling the temple (2Ch. 5:12–13; 1Ki. 8:10–11). Whether it was

the reading of the Law or worship in the synagogue or temple, the people sang and worshipped God with joy (2Ch. 29:25–30; Ezr. 3:10–11). Even the prophets challenged the people to sing praises joyfully to the Lord (Isa. 12:5; 42:10; Jer. 20:13; Zec. 2:10).

The whole assembly of worship is done in families. Even the family of Levites was designated as priests and worship leaders for Israel. David assigned 4,000 Levitical musicians to praise God on instruments made specifically "for giving praise" (1Ch. 23:5). Families are not only to teach their children to play musical instruments for the purpose of worship, but people are awakening to the idea that praise and worship happens in families, not just presenting the best singers or musicians within the worshiping community.

When Messiah came, He said to a Samaritan woman, "You worship that which you do not know; we worship that which we know, for salvation is from the Jews (John 4:22). David writes of a time when all the nations will worship God and "shout joyfully, while serving the Lord with gladness" (e.g. Psalm 67; 86, and 100).

One reads in Revelation 15:4 where "all the nations shall come and worship before God" because of the slain, resurrected, and exalted Lamb of God.[3] The Messiah is depicted as a King on a throne (Rev. 5). Worship begins with seeing the King!

The Victory of Community

Some pupils came to the Rabbi complaining about the prevalence of evil in the world. They asked the Rabbi how they might drive out the darkness. The Rabbi gave them brooms and asked them to sweep the darkness from the cellar. The pupils tried this, but they were not successful. So the Rabbi gave them sticks and told them to beat the darkness until it was driven away. Again they tried, and when they failed, the Rabbi asked them to try shouting at the darkness. The pupils did this also, but the darkness remained. "Then let us try this," the Rabbi said, "let each person challenge the darkness by lighting a candle." The pupils descended into the cellar. Each one lit a candle. When they looked about, they discovered that the darkness had disappeared.

Isaiah 49:6*c* says, "I will… make you (Israel) a light for the nations (Gentiles), that you may bring salvation to the ends of the earth." God's people are called to be a distinct people who live in the power of God's victory over the powers of evil. All of Scripture is in the context of community. For Israel, the synagogue is the rallying center for worship and a place of prayer, where people gather to hear the Torah read. Every detail of life is to be controlled by Torah.

According to Jewish tradition, "Moses received the Torah on Sinai, and handed it down to Joshua; Joshua to the Elders; the Elders to the Prophets; and the Prophets handed it down to the men of the Great Assembly."[1] We even see a similar pattern in the early church that handed down apostolic tradition in which apostolic succession came to be a sign for God's people of "unity" under the authority of God's Word.[2]

We also see in Scripture a divided Israel into northern and southern kingdoms. Nowhere do we see God referring to His people as "Israels." This division was a kind of divine suffering which even the church today suffers under a similar discipline. God desires a penitent people, but could it be through these many fragmentations — and even the separation of Israel from the church — that God "has torn us to pieces that He might heal us"(Hos. 6:1)?

The word of the Lord came to Haggai saying, "Is it a time for you yourselves to be living in paneled houses, while this house remains a ruin?" (Hag. 1:4). Then the people took wood up to the hills and built the house and God was pleased and manifested His glory. God is saying today, "Is it a time for you yourselves to dwell in your 'churches' while the Son's body is still divided?" God is calling Jews and Gentiles together as one family that illuminates the whole world with the fire of God's reconciling love.

As one who has been reading the Bible in one hand and the Talmud in the other hand, there are several important things to understand about discerning the body and coming together to worship in community. The first is the realization that the community is foremost a place of continually giving thanks to God. This is a central part of not only synagogue worship but is the heart and breath of Christian worship in thanking God for loving the world by sending the Messiah. This is a community of joy and delight. God calls His people to discover the treasures of true delight in Him.

It is also important to understand that the Jewish Passover had taken place in two different times and in two different places — in the temple and in the home. In houses of worship, God's people offer themselves as a living sacrifice in praise and celebration, in brokenness and repentance. The family is central to the life of the Jewish people as is the health and spiritual vitality of the spiritual family of God. God's generational blessings to families can even extend to the thousand generation.[3]

Holy living and worship in Israel resolved around the Passover that consecrated the people. Similarly, it's the Eucharist life before God that consecrates families and the church. The Eucharist life which celebrates God's atonement for the people's sins by the gift of His Son is where all of God's people no matter where they find themselves, totally abandon themselves to the Father's will as Jesus did Himself.[4] God's presence which up to now had been manifested in a cloud of glory — an elusive glory that came and went — now manifests itself in God's Spirit inhabiting His people.

Israel has always maintained a marriage imagery, with God as the Bridegroom and they as His Bride. In the Messiah, God's transformed — and ever transforming — community recognizes Jesus as the Bridegroom and the church is His bride. This Messianic community is God's new social order, where people's hearts are so captivated by Yeshua/Jesus that they are like Jesus to the world.[5] It is the reconciled community of Jews and Gentiles, Israel and the church together that will capture the attention of a world that has lost sight of what genuine community and unity truly looks like.

> There is a story that is told of a monastery that had fallen upon hard times. Once a great order, but now hardly anyone came to the monastery anymore. The younger Rabbi asked a visiting older Rabbi if he had any advice for him and the few others who kept up the monastery. The Rabbi quietly said, "There is only one thing I have to tell you: one of you is the Messiah." When the young Rabbi returned to greet his fellow monks at the monastery they asked him, "What did the visiting Rabbi say?" The young Rabbi said, "He only had one thing to say as he was leaving. He said that one of us was the Messiah." As the days and weeks and months followed, the monks began to think about the visiting Rabbi's words and wondered if they could actually be true? "The Messiah is one of us? If that is the case, who is it? Did he mean one of the other monks? Could the Rabbi have meant me? I'm just an ordinary person but supposed he did. What if I am the Messiah?" As all the monks contemplated the matter, they all began to treat each other with extraordinary respect on the off chance that one of them might actually be the Messiah. And on the off, off chance that each member himself might be the Messiah, they began to treat themselves with extraordinary care. As time went by, people visiting the monastery noticed the respect and gentle kindness that surrounded the old monks of this small congregation. Occasional visitors found themselves deeply moved by the life of the monks. Before long, people were coming from far and wide to be spiritually nourished by the contagious life of these monks. They began to bring their friends, and their friends brought more friends. Within a few years, the small congregation was once again a thriving order, thanks to the old visiting Rabbi's words, a vibrant center of life and spirit.

❋ | *The* Victory *of* Peace

Rabbi Meir would comment on the Torah every day and there was a woman who came and listened to him attentively each time. In fact, the woman's husband was a jealous and ill tempered and was angry with her for giving him his supper late. "Where have you been?" he demanded, although he knew perfectly well that she have been to the Rabbi's talk. "Please forgive me" she replied. "I'm sorry I was late, I attended Rabbi Meir lecture, and his words were so inspiring that I lost track of time."Since you apparently love being with your Rabbi so much" he yelled at her, "I order you to go back to him this instant and spit in his face as payment for his wonderful talk. Don't set foot back in this house until you have done so." "But that's impossible!" she pleaded. "Is it not a wife's duty, according to the law espoused by your Rabbi, to do as her husband tells her?" he insisted. "Yes, but — ." "Then do as I say!" he shouted, and he forced her out of the house. At a loss, the woman went to the home of one of her good friend's, who offered her a place to sleep for the night. The next morning, hoping that her husband had cooled off, she tried to return home. But he was adamant and refused to let her into the house until she had spit in the Rabbi's face. Meanwhile her friend had gone to Rabbi Meir and explained the woman's predicament. Immediately the good Rabbi sent for the woman. When she arrived, he pretended to have a speck of dust in his eye. "I think I have something in my eye," he told her. "Do you know of anything that might help?" "I'm not sure, Rabbi," she answered, concerned for his discomfort. "I have heard it said," he replied, "that such a pain can be relieved if a good woman spits into it seven times. Please, would you do me the kindness of spitting into my eye?" She hesitated, but the Rabbi insisted. And so, in the presence of the Rabbi's disciples, the woman spit seven times into his eye."Thank you," he said to her. "It is much better. Go now, and inform your husband that you have spit in the face of Rabbi Meir, not once, as he ordered, but seven times." The woman realized what the Rabbi had done for her, offered him a thousand thanks, and went home. There she was reunited with her husband, who, having realized the kindness and the wisdom of the Rabbi Meir, begged his wife's forgiveness. After she had left, the Rabbi's students turned to him and said, "Master, how could you permit such an indignity? It's unthinkable!" "Don't you see?" he answered in his gentle voice. "Apart from an act of outright cruelty, there can be no indignity in doing something that brings peace between two people."

The stability and joy of a community rests on peace. The Talmud says, "By three things is the world preserved: by truth, by judgment, and by peace; as it is said, 'Judge ye the truth the judgment of peace in your gates'" (Zec. 8:16).[1] For where there is no peace, there is neither prosperity nor well being. Even the rabbinic prayers begin and end with prayers for giving and receiving peace. God's intention from the beginning was for His creation to be blessed with peace.[2] The Talmud says:

> *Mankind was first created as a single individual because of the various families which have issued from him, that they should not quarrel one with the other. Since now there is so much strife although he was created one, how much more so if there had been two created![3]*

God's calls all of His people to the pathway of peace and to His peaceable Kingdom. God's shalom of peace makes us into peacemakers. One of Hillel's favorite maxims was "Be of the disciples of Aaron, loving peace and pursuing peace."[4] How is one to be a lover of peace? The Talmud teaches, "that a man must love peace to abide in Israel among all individuals in the same way that Aaron loved peace to abide among all individuals; as it is said, 'The law of truth was in his mouth; he walked with Me in peace and uprightness and did turn many away from iniquity'" (Mal. 2:6).[5]

The Talmud also says that the Messiah will inaugurate a time of abiding peace.[6] Jesus imitated God just as all Jews rightly strive to do. To be like Jesus requires that the community of faith practiced virtues like Jesus. The cross summarized His whole life and the church and all of God's people are called to be a cruciform people.[7] God's peaceable Kingdom is one of a nonviolent life. Israel and all who follow God are to walk in the way of the Lord and imitate God through the prophets (Torah), the King (Son-ship), and the Priest (spiritual knowledge). In Jesus' life, we see anew God's way with Israel and subsequently what it means for Israel to be God's beloved.

God's Kingdom is present in His people, which reveals the effective power of God to create a new alternative community capable of living peaceable in a violent world. God's people are to embody God's Kingdom virtues of peace, righteousness, and justice. God's peace ultimately leads people to peace with Him, ourselves, and with one another. What we see in revelation is God does not rule creation through coercion but through the cross.[8]

The task of Christian people is not to seek to control history, but to be faithful to the mode of life of the peaceable Kingdom. No conversation over differences is more important than that between Israel and the Church. For it is from the Church that we learn of the God who is present to us in the life, cross, and resurrection of Jesus. It is from Israel's continuing willingness to wait for the Messiah that we learn better how we must wait between the times. The church and Israel are two people walking in the path provided by God; they cannot walk independently of one another, for if they do they both risk becoming lost.[9]

There is a powerful rabbinic legend, "A Rabbi was standing in a marketplace when Elijah appeared to him. The Rabbi asked him, "Is there anybody in this market-place who will have his share in the World to Come?" Elijah answered there was not. In the meanwhile there came two men, and Elijah said, "These will have a share in the World to Come." The Rabbi asked them, "What is your occupation?" They answered, "We are merrymakers; when we see men troubled in mind we cheer them, and when we see two men quarreling, we make peace between them."

❀ | *The* Victory *of* Wisdom

A Roman noblewoman approached the Rabbi and asked, "What sense can be made from the saying: 'God gives wisdom to the wise'? Shouldn't it say: 'God gives wisdom to the foolish'? The Rabbi replied, 'Do you have any jewelry'?" "Yes," the noblewoman responded. "And if two people came to borrow your jewelry — one rich and the other poor — to whom would you lend your valuable?" "Oh," she replied, "to the one who is rich." "And why?" "Because the one who is rich would be able to pay for the jewels should they be lost or stolen. One who is poor, on the other hand, could not." "Likewise," the Rabbi said, "God gives wisdom to the wise, and not to fools."

Jewish wisdom tradition originated in the understanding that God and wisdom were together from the beginning.[1] Judaism came to identify wisdom with the Torah. There is a parable in the Talmud that says:

> ...concerning *"a person who is standing in darkness but has a lamp in his hand. He sees a stone but does not stumble over it. He sees a drain but does not fall into it, because he has a lamp in his hand; as it is said, 'Thy word is a lamp unto my feet, and a light unto my path.* (Psa. 119:105)[2]

God's wisdom therefore became associated with God's Torah (*Logos*). In the New Testament, Jesus not only possessed wisdom or was a wise man, but He was God's wisdom incarnate: the Word (*Logos*) made flesh.[3]

It is true, there is a difference between the way Yeshua/Jesus handled Jewish tradition and the way the religious leaders of His time did. When Jesus spoke of God's Word or the Law, He spoke about it in His own name, rather than the usual citation of other Jewish authorities to back one's claims. He was famous for saying, "You have heard it said… but I say to you…" (Mat. 5:21–22,27,31,33,38, etc.). The prophets would ask God to help and give the Jewish people rest, where Jesus said, "Come to me, all of you that are weary and are carrying heavy burdens, and I will give you rest" (Mat. 11:28).

The Rabbis could say that if two or three men sat together, having said the words of Torah, the *shekinah* (God's own glorious presence) would dwell with them. Jesus said, "Where two or three are gathered in my name, I am there among them" (Mat. 18:20).[4] Jesus is simply not a spokesman for wisdom, He is the wisdom of God, He is the Torah (*Logos*) in person. Jesus is the One Whose death on a cross bridged the gap between man's foolishness and God's wisdom and eternal plans. The cross represents the very intersection and unity God will restore in destiny, bringing together Israel and the church.

> In a certain city there lived an influential man whose heart was full of hatred toward the Jews. One day he came up with an evil plan. He summoned the chief Rabbi 1and declared, "It is my wish to have a debate with a Jew, any Jew of your choosing, and the Jew you select for the debate must understand sign language of my choosing, and the Jew you select for the debate must understand every sign that I make. If no one can be found to take part in the debate, your entire community will be put to the sword. You have thirty days to prepare. Now be gone!" The Rabbi's words to the other Jews sent them into a terrible state of despair. How could any Jew understand the arbitrary sign language of this influential and powerful man? The Rabbi ordered everyone to fast and pray for God to deliver them. This fast went on for four weeks and there was no Jew who came forward to debate this evil man. There was, however, this simple poultry dealer, a good but simple man, who had been away on business and had just returned from a long trip. He had no idea what had transpired and found his whole community in a month long fast. When they told him what had happened, he went to the Rabbi and told him he would be willing to debate this man who wanted to kill his people. At that point, the Rabbi was so desperate and was willing to take anyone, so he consented to this simple poultry dealer to debate the evil man. The hour of the debate had arrived and the man was pleased that the Jews had sent such a simpleton to debate him. He told him, "You must understand every one of my signs and if you fail to follow correctly even a single one of them, I shall know your people are ignorant and all their lives will be forfeited." The man began the debate by silently pointing one finger at the poultry dealer. Carefully reading the sign, the Jew responded by pointing two fingers back at the man. The man then reached into his pocket and pulled out a slice of cheddar cheese. The poul-

try dealer removed an egg from his own pocket. At that, the man took a handful of grain and scattered it across the floor. Without a moment's hesitation, the poultry dealer released a hen from a coop he had brought a long, and the hen ate up all the grain. "I can not believe it!" the man said, "You replied correctly to every question I put to you. I now realize that if such a simple man among you can understand these signs, you Jews must truly be wise and chosen of God. I have been wrong about you. Please forgive me." Meanwhile everyone in the Jewish community heard about the poultry dealer winning the debate and the Rabbi was astounded and wanted to know how the poultry dealer did it? He went to him and asked him, "How did you understand his signs?" "It was quite simple, really," the poultry dealer answered. "First he pointed at me with one finger, which meant that he was going to poke out my eye. I answered by pointing at him with two fingers, to let him know that if he tried that, I would poke out both of his eyes. Next he took out a piece of cheese to show that, while I was hungry, he was the one who had the food. So just to prove to him that I had no need of his charity, I took out an egg. Finally he threw a handful of grain on the floor. Why, I admit, I don't know. But I did know that it was feeding time for my hen, and I thought it would be a pity to waste the grain. So I let my hen out of her coop, and she ate up the grain. The next thing I know, I was walking home the victor!" "Truly God has been merciful!" The Rabbi said in relief. While the Rabbi was listening to the poultry dealer, the man who lost the debate was talking to his friends and they asked him, "How did the debate go and are you going to have the Jews exterminated?" "Not at all," said the man. "Never have I come across such a wise and holy people. You see, I began by pointing at the Jew with one finger to indicate that there is only one King. He answered by pointing at me with two fingers, declaring that there are in fact two Kings — one in heaven and one on earth — which of course he was right. "Next I pulled a piece of cheddar cheese from my pocket to ask him, 'Is this cheese made from white or black goat milk?' But the Jew was not easily fooled by such a ploy. In reply to the question, the clever man produced an egg which was to ask, 'Does this egg come from a white or brown hen?' "I thought I could trick him by changing the subject. So I spread some grain on the floor as a sign that the Jews are spread out all over the world. That wise and humble man, however, released his hen from his coop, and the hen ate up all the grain. That meant that the Messiah would come and gather all the Jews from exile and return them to the Holy Land. I realized that I had no choice but to acknowledge the man's wisdom and spare his people."

And so the Scripture is fulfilled, "for the foolishness of God is greater than the wisdom of man" (1Cor. 1:25).

❧ | *The* Messiah's Victory

Many years ago a fugitive entered a small village and attempted to hide there from the authorities. The people, not knowing that he was a wanted man, were kind and generous. They provided for him and opened their hearts in hospitality. In fact, in time, they accepted him as one of their own. They grew to love him. One afternoon a group of soldiers entered the village in search of the fugitive. They were certain the young man was hiding somewhere among the people. When no one offered to help the soldiers, or provide them with information about the fugitive, the soldiers grew angry. They threatened to kill the people and burn the village unless the young man was handed over to them. The people were torn; they did not know what to do. They went to the village Rabbi and asked him for his advice. The Rabbi was troubled. On the one hand he did not want to deliver the young man over to the authorities and a certain death. But on the other hand he did not want see his people and the village destroyed. And so he decided to seek guidance through prayer by searching the Scriptures. All night long he read the Bible and prayed. Finally, as dawn was breaking, he happened upon these words from the Bible: "It is better that one man dies than that the whole people be lost." Upon reading this, the Rabbi closed the Bible and called the soldiers. He told them where the young man was hiding. After the soldiers found the young man, they led him away to be killed, and the entire village joined together in a celebration, praising the Rabbi because he had saved the people from destruction. However, the Rabbi, overcome with deep sadness because a human life had been taken, retired to his room and did not join the others in the celebration. That night and angel of God visited the Rabbi. The angel appeared to him and asked, "What have you done?" The Rabbi answered, "I handed over the fugitive to the enemy." "But you have handed over the Messiah!" The Rabbi cried, "How could I have known?" The angel answered, "If, instead of reading the Scriptures and praying, you had taken the time to visit the young man and look once into his eyes, you would have known."

Moses says in Deuteronomy 18:15,17–8: "The Lord your God will raise up for you a prophet like Me from among your own brothers... The Lord said to me... I will raise up for them a prophet like you from among their brothers." Just as God raised up Moses, so He would raise up a future prophet for the people of Israel like Moses. But the problem is that Deuteronomy 34:10–11 says:

> *Since then, no prophet has risen in Israel like Moses, whom the Lord knew face to face, who did all those miraculous signs and wonders... For no one has ever shown the mighty power or performed the awesome deeds that Moses did in the sight of all Israel.*

The question now is, "Where, then, is the prophet like Moses? Where is the one who will work signs and wonders and deliver God's people from bondage and sin?" The Jewish people of the first century believed this great prophet would be the one they called "Messiah."

The Messiah is to bring peace and reconciliation and forgiveness to the world. It is even taught in the Talmud by the school of Elijah that "The world will endure six thousand years — two thousand years in chaos, two thousand years with Torah, and two thousand years will be the days of the Messiah."[1] The first two thousand years means from the time of Adam to Abraham. The two thousand years of the Torah means from Abraham to around the beginning of the common era. The Messianic age roughly consists of the last two thousand years. The Talmud goes on to say that because people's iniquities were many, the Messiah did not come at the expected time. Is it possible that the Messiah did come two thousand years ago, but "because our iniquities were many," many people from the line of Abraham did not recognize Him?

The Talmud further states, "If [the people of Israel] are worthy [the Messiah] will come 'with the clouds of heaven' (Dan. 7:13); if they are not worthy, 'lowly and riding upon a donkey' (Zec. 9:9)." Shortly before He died, Yeshua/Jesus entered Jerusalem riding a donkey, with the crowds hailing Him as the Messiah. But then the people turned upon Him. Is it possible that He came "lowly and riding a donkey" because we were not worthy of His coming, and in the future, when we recognize Him as the Messiah, He will return in the clouds of heaven?[2]

The whole foundation of the sacrificial system was built upon Messianic beliefs; the Messiah would be like a new high priest, to make intercession and atonement for the nation. The whole Hebrew Bible points to the Messiah, for Whom many Jews are still waiting.

Jesus said, "Everything must be fulfilled that is written about me in the law of Moses, the prophets, and the Psalms" (Luke 24:44).[3] He predicted the terrible destruction of Jerusalem and the temple, warning people of the consequences of rejecting His words.[4] Many Jewish believers and people with Abrahamic ancestry are now coming to faith in Jesus because of His fulfillment of Messianic prophecies.[5] Everything from Yeshua/Jesus birth, miraculous deeds, suffering, death, and resurrection are prophesized in the Hebrew Bible.[6] Acts 2:29–32 says:

> *Brothers, I can tell you confidently that the patriarch David died and was buried, and his tomb is here to this day. But he was a prophet and knew God had promised him on oath that he would place one of his descendants on his throne. Seeing what was ahead, he spoke of the resurrection of the [Messiah], that he was not abandoned to the grave, nor did his body see decay. God raised this Jesus to life, and we are all witnesses of the fact.*

The Messiah was a divine man who brought the presence of God (the *shekinah*) to earth two thousand years ago and will return with divine glory in the future. The Scriptures teach that Yahweh Himself had to literally visit the Second Temple (according to Mal. 3) and will return literally and stand on the mount of Olives in the future (Zec. 14).[7]

Who else has fulfilled all the Messianic prophecies if not Yeshua/Jesus? Who else has come in the demonstration of signs and wonder and God's power if not Jesus? Who else has brought forgiveness and reconciliation between people and nations if not Jesus? Jesus is the world's most famous Jew and even world history is now divided into years before and after His birth.

Almost one third of the world — two billion people, Jews and Gentles alike — claims to follow this Messiah King. It will be no surprise to many of Yeshua's followers when their Messiah is not only a light to all the nations, which is actually being fulfilled in our day, but will return in the clouds and establish His holy Kingdom of *shalom* (peace) forever. We stand at the very threshold of God's destiny for all of humanity and His beloved creation.

❀ | *The* Victory *of the* Kingdom

Everyone knew that it was impossible for even the most learned of Rabbis to defeat Rabbi Naftali in an argument. But on one occasion, on the eve of Simchat Torah, the people were dancing in celebrating all the blessings they receive from the Torah. When Rabbi Naftali joined in the festivities, he noticed among the Hasidim a coachman who was known to be so ignorant that some thought he was illiterate. "What are you doing here?" the Rabbi challenged him. "You never study Torah, and you break half of its commandments. What can this celebration held in the observance of the Torah mean to you?" "But Rabbi, the sages teach us that the tablets of the Torah are like a bride and groom," the coachman surprised the rabbi with an allusion to the Midrash. "If my brother arranges a wedding, am I not allowed to participate in the celebrations?" "Indeed you are," the Rabbi smiled, pleased at the man's insight. "Dance on! For you have defeated me!"

The Rabbis taught that submission to divine discipline and holy living defined what it means to accept "the yoke of the Kingdom of Heaven."[1] The Kingdom of God and Kingdom of Heaven are used interchangeably throughout Scripture, representing God's rule and authority over all creation. Righteous conduct established the Kingdom of God.[2]

There is a Rabbinic saying: "Physical cleanliness leads to spiritual purity." It was therefore taught by the Rabbis, "Whoever wishes to receive upon himself the yoke of the Kingdom of Heaven in perfection should first wash his hands, put on the phylacteries (the Scriptures on the body), and offer his prayers."[3] Physical cleansing represents the spiritual cleansing of God's Kingdom.[4] God's people are to line themselves up with God's invisible and spiritual Kingdom, which is more substantial and real than the things seen in the physical universe around us.

The book of Hebrews is a significant book, connecting both testaments and the real (spiritual) world to the types and shadows of the physical world (Heb. .8–10). The Kingdom does not come as we think, nor can it be domesticated by man's ways or thoughts. In many ways, the Kingdom of God is a reversal of our world that had been so wounded, demonized, and turned upside down.[5]

The Kingdom of God is the work and reign of God.[6] The Hebrew Bible does not so much speak of a Kingdom of God as it reminds us that God is King. To speak of "the Kingdom of God" is to remind ourselves that God is the Sovereign Lord: "the earth is the Lord's and the fullness thereof" (Psa. 24:1).

The Scriptures refer to the Messiah Who is the Anointed Son of the King. He is "the Word made flesh," preaching and announcing the sudden arrival of God's Kingdom on earth. Jesus came preaching and teaching the Kingdom of God. Jesus taught that "the secret of the Kingdom has been given to you" (Mark 4:11; Mat. 13:11; Luke 8:10). The hidden Kingdom is now revealed and the Kingdom is both present and future, earthly and heavenly.[7]

The Apostle Paul speaks of "the mystery of the Gospel" (Eph. 6: 19), "the mystery of Christ" (Col. 4:3), and "the mystery of godliness" (1Ti. 3:16). God's unfolding plans and revelation culminates in the life, death, and resurrection of the Messiah, Who reconciles creation and animates the messianic community (Rom. 16:24–26; 1Cor. 2:7–10; Col. 1:26–27; and 1Ti. 3:16). This hidden Kingdom is being manifested in "the new reconciled man in Christ," in whom Israel and the church are yoked together as one people of God (Eph. 2:14–18; Rom. 11:24).

Jews and Gentiles are brought together in God's economy and Kingdom, which was once hidden, but is now revealed in the Messiah. Ethics of God's Kingdom and economy direct and rule the lives of God's people. Where the world has subverted so much of God's messianic people, so Jesus Spirit and power comes to subvert the world with the ethics and practices of God's Kingdom.[8]

The Messiah came the first time not as a conquering king, but one clothed in humility and weakness. God revealed His divine love in that mystery and in Yeshua's embrace of the cross. Kingdom ethics therefore become crucifixion ethics. The messianic community is a community of the cross which lays down its life for the sake of others. It is only in coming to the end of ourselves that we discover that God's strength is made perfect in our weakness (2Cor. 12:9).

It is through the self-giving powerlessness of Yeshua/Jesus that God gives His messianic community the power Jesus had to heal the sick, to call the dead to life, to reconcile the estranged, and to build the

Kingdom of God. As the Kingdom starts small and hidden and grows, the sign of God's Kingdom is God's people living as an alternative society bringing justice and righteousness to everyone around them.

Philip Yancey describes this new Messianic community and Kingdom of God advancing on the world with these words. The Kingdom of God is:

> ...a society that welcomes people of all races and social classes, that is characterized by love and not polarization, that cares most for its weakest members, that stands for justice and righteousness in a world enamored with selfishness and decadence, a society in which members compete for the privilege of serving one another — this is what Jesus meant by the kingdom of God.[9]

Jesus Himself is an agent and sign of God's eternal Kingdom. Jesus miracles were not proof-texts or scientific evidence for God's Kingdom, but were signposts and markers of the arrival of God's Kingdom. Everything He said and did was announcing the reign of God.[10] "Jesus healings are not supernatural miracles in a natural world. They are the only truly 'natural' things in a world that is unnatural, demonized, and wounded."[11] God, through His Messiah, has turned the world right-side back up. We, who have been far off, are brought close to the day where all the kingdoms of this world become the Kingdom of the Messiah and He will reign forever and forever (Rev. 11:15).

> There was a great wedding festival. Friends of the family wanted to spread joy and blessing, so they invited everyone from the village to join them in the celebration. In one corner of their large home they set up a place for a group of musicians to play. Soon the entire house was filled with music, dancing, and rejoicing. As they were dancing, a deaf man passed by the front window of the house. He could see people leaping about, whirling around the room, and waving their arms in the air, but he could not see the musicians or hear the music. Thus he declared to himself, 'Look at all that commotion! This must be a house full of madmen!' And so the poor man went on his way, unable to take part in the celebration. For he could not hear the music that animated the wedding guests.

The Victory of the Spirit

"Know that God never leaves off speaking to us," Rabbi Abraham Yaakov Friedman of Sadgora would declare to his disciples. "Not only in the works of nature does He call out to us but also in the works of humanity. For those who are created in the image of their Creator participate in His creation. Which means: their works are part of His utterance." There was a young man among the Rabbi's disciples who had complete faith in the truth of his teacher's every word. No sooner would an utterance come from the Rabbi's lips than the student would examine it, wrestle with it, and struggle to learn from it. But he had a great deal of trouble with this particular teaching, especially when he looked around and saw the work in which some people were engaged. So one day the young man gathered his courage and went to the Rabbi to question him about this teaching. "Rabbi," he said, "if you will forgive me, there is something I must ask you." "Please ask," Abraham Yaakov replied, always glad to have a question from one of his students. "You have told us that God addresses us in everything," he continued, "both in the wonders of nature and in the actions of man. But when I look around at the new inventions that have come into the world, I cannot see anything of value to be learned from them. The railroads that cut across the land foul the air with their smoke and their noise. The telephone removes us from the face of our neighbor. And the telegraph reduces words — the most holy of things — to mere dots and dashes. What can God possibly be teaching us through these things?" The Rabbi smiled patiently at the young man's concern and answered, "Oh, but the Holy One, blessed be He, is offering us His wisdom even through these new inventions. You may have noticed that people who tarry in idleness often miss the train. So you see, the railroad teaches us that a moment's hesitation will cause us to miss everything. As for the telephone, it enables us to speak with others over long distances. Therefore it reminds us that what is said here is heard there. And the telegraph? Here we have

perhaps the most important lesson of all. The telegraph teaches us that every word is counted — and charged. Thus even in these new strange inventions God is speaking to us." And, hearing these words of his teacher, the young man could hear God's voice where he had thought there to be nothing.

The Holy Spirit (*Ruach Hakodesh*) in Jewish thought was something that came on and went from the prophets and specially anointed people of God. God's Holy Spirit, in Jewish thought, is associated both with God's nearness and the gift of prophecy. Prophecy was to cease when the Messiah would come, for all Israel was to be prophets according to Joel 2:28.[1]

The Spirit of God endowed people with many gifts and abilities Solomon had the spirit of wisdom; Daniel, one of understanding and counsel; Moses with the Spirit's power and might; Elijah the fear of the Lord; and Isaiah with spiritual discernment and insight. Even David, a man after God's own heart, was endowed by the Spirit with gifts of music and prophecy.

The Spirit of God creates and energizes all of life. Psalm 33:6 says, "By the word of the Lord the heavens were established, and all their power by His Spirit." We see in Jewish thought the connection between the Spirit, wisdom, and creation in Christian thought.[2] There is a similar progression and development from God "tabernacling" with His people, from the ark to the temple and the promise of God wanting to get even closer by tabernacling within His people. Ezekiel 37 is a promise of God putting His Spirit within you so that you shall live.[3]

In the New Testament, we see that where the church is, there is the Spirit of God, and where the Spirit of God is, there is the church of the living God.

> *In Rabbinic theology, there was a widespread notion that the Spirit of God had dwelt in the first temple, but had been lost in the second, only to be restored in the temple of the end of time... This strong understanding of the last days also filled the early Christian community's self-understanding as the Spirit-filled temple... According to the Rabbis, the Spirit indwelling the temple was prophetic in nature... Barnabas 16:6–10 says, "And it shall come to pass when the [last] week is ended that a temple of God shall be built... God truly dwells in us, in the habitation which we are. How? His word of faith, the calling of His promise, the wisdom of the ordinances, the commands of the teaching, Himself prophesying in us, Himself dwelling in us... This is a spiritual temple being built for the Lord.*[4]

The revelation of God gets clearer-and-clearer until a composite picture begins to unfold or be unveiled. God's spiritual temple is being built every day as more and more people enter into God's Kingdom, both Gentiles and Jews, turning to the God of Israel through Yeshua/Jesus the Messiah. God's Spirit empowers and renews, cleanses and indwells (inhabits) the people of God.

We are now living in the days of the Messiah and His Kingdom. The New Testament says, "But now in [Messiah] Jesus, you who once were far away have been brought near through the blood of the [Messiah]" (Eph. 2:12–13). The writer goes onto explain that Jesus "came and preached peace to you who were far away and peace to those who were near. Through Him we both have access to the Father by one Spirit (Eph. 2:17–18).

What we see in history and Scripture, through the providence of God, that God is building a worldwide spiritual temple consisting of both redeemed Gentiles and redeemed Jews. The earthly and the spiritual temple, as well as the earthly and the spiritual Jerusalem, come together — ancient Jewish thought teaches that the temple will one day descend to earth.

Throughout Jewish history, we see the manifest presence and glory of God, which is to find its fulfillment and culmination in the glory and splendor of the Messiah. It is the Messiah Who ushers into the world the age of God's manifest glory and the abiding, indwelling, everlasting presence of Almighty God.

> *The Rabbi once had a dream of paradise. He entered by being dunked in a deep well, and when he came out, he saw only a few saints sitting at tables and studying the Torah. The Rabbi asked the accompanying angel, "Is this all there is to paradise?" The angel answered, "You seem to think that the saints are in paradise. But you have it backwards. Paradise is in the saints."*

❀ | *The* Victory *of* Faith

Four sages determined that they would enter into the garden of the Divine Mysteries. They were Ben Azzai, Ben Zoma, Elisha ben Abuyah, and Rabbi Akiva. As they were making their preparations, Rabbi Akiva warned his comrades, "When you approach the stones of pure marble in the palace of the Holy One, blessed be He, do not be afraid, even though they may look like a wall of water ready to engulf you. Do not cry out, 'Water! Water!' For it is written, 'He that speaks falsehood will not be established before My eyes.' Therefore, if you would draw nigh unto God, you must do so in truth and faith. Do you understand? In truth and in faith!" Having spoken these words, Rabbi Akiva spoke no more. He and the other sages proceeded. When Ben Azzai entered into the holy realm, however, the vision of God's palace was too much for him. As he drew near the pillars of white, he was convinced that he was about to drown. But before he could shout, 'Water! Water!' he perished. Thus in the Scriptures it is written, "Precious in the sight of the Lord is the death of His saints." After Ben Azzai came Ben Zoma. But he too failed to heed the warning of Rabbi Akiva. Confusing the pure marble for water, he fell into a state of absolute confusion and went mad. Thus in the Scriptures it is written, "Have you found honey? Eat only as much as you need, lest you be filled to overflowing and vomit it up." Then came Elisha ben Abuyah, who also believed the deception of his eyes rather than the truth of Akiva's words. Unlike his comrades, however, he succumbed neither to death nor to madness but fell prey to a fate far worse: He lost his faith — which he, perhaps, never had, since it is through faith that the eyes behold marble instead of water — and became an apostate. Forever thereafter he was known as Acher, the alien Other. Rabbi Akiva, so great was his faith, entered the garden without mistaking the pure marble for water. He alone entered in peace and departed in peace. For Rabbi Akiva alone entered in truth and in faith.

Man is neither the Lord of the universe nor master of his own destiny. Man does not posses God, but God possesses man. God's divine ownership frees us to see the beauty of God, the power of His love, and the mystery of faith which is a gift from God. Faith is like the bridge between the heart of man and the love of God. It is through faith that one finds communion with God.

For the Jews, to believe is to remember. The whole Jewish faith is one of remembering past encounters with God, with glimpses of God's presence, peace, and power in the present. The Jewish faith is a recollection of the stories and experiences which occurred to and through her ancestors.[1]

Faith, in the Jewish mind, is not something just intellectual or that demands proof, but is a humble, devoted, and sacrificial mind and heart for the true and living God. Faith sees the invisible, believes the impossible, and tastes the sacred and intangible. Ultimately, faith is the risk of commitment.[2] Faith loves, sacrifices, and surrenders, even in the face of persecution and death.

The Rabbis point out that faith is the distinguishing feature of the lives and heroes of the Hebrew Bible.[3] Israel received the favor of God because of faith. Similarly, you find that Father Abraham inherited the world and the world to come by virtue of faith, as it is said, "He believed in the Lord, and He counted it to him for righteousness" (Gen. 15:6).

Throughout the Scriptures, there is a dynamic tension and relationship between faith and obedience. The apostle Paul, in Romans, speaks of "the obedience that comes from faith" (1:5). Jews and Christians believe that "obedience (to God) leads to righteousness" (Rom. 6:16).

Grace and law, faith and obedience all find their fulfillment in the Messiah, Who "through the obedience of the one man the many will be made righteous" (Rom. 5:19). When the Messiah returns, Jesus says God will be looking for people with faith (Luke 18:8).

One of the hallmarks of Scripture is "the righteous will live by faith" (Hab. 2:4; Rom. 1:7; Gal. 3:11; Heb. 10:38). Faith fills the believer with the desire to do the will of God. "For without faith, it is impossible to please God" (Heb. 11:6). Biblical faith always leads to repentance and obedience.

All the heroes of the Bible showed their faith by obedience. True faith produces righteous works.[4] Believers are instructed "to work out your salvation with fear and trembling, for it is God who works in you to will and act according to His good purpose" (Php. 2:12–13).

Acts 6:7 shows how the early church understood a faith that works: "A great many... were becoming obedient to the faith." The great "faith chapter" in the book of Hebrews says, "By faith... Abraham obeyed" (11:8). Obedience is the inevitable result of biblical faith. Righteous living is expressed as the result of real faith (Rom. 10:10). The book of James says that true faith produces the fruit of righteousness. Faith without works is dead and useless (2:17,20). Faith provides: perseverance in trials (1:1–12), obedience to the Word of God (1:13–25), and righteous works (2:14–26). It tames the tongue (3:1–12), gives true wisdom (3:13–18), brings humility and submission to God (3:7–17), and godly behavior in the community of faith (5:1–20).[5]

> *"Forgive me, Rabbi" a disciple said, "but there is something I must ask you. I know we are taught that God is always near, closer to us than our own shadows. But I must confess to you that there are times when the Infinite One seems to be infinitely far. Can you help me with this?" The Rabbi thought for a moment and then replied, "Have you ever watched a father teach his child how to walk? For a while he will hold the toddler by the hand and walk at his side, guiding him and encouraging him every step of the way. But there comes a time when the father will let go, so that the little fellow may try to walk on his own toward him. It may be frightening at first, but soon they give each other a loving embrace, and then the father moves back again. Each time the child steps toward his father by himself he learns to walk a little better. Know, then, that God, who is Father of all, teaches us to walk in the same manner. He moves away from us for a time, so that we may move toward Him. Moving towards Him, we learn to move toward life.*

The Victory *of* Restoration

When the Babylonians were about to destroy the Temple, the Holy One, blessed be He, gazed down from on high and saw our father Abraham standing at the Temple alter. He said, "Why have you, my beloved, come to stand in My house?" "I have come," Abraham replied, "because I am concerned about the fate of my children. Where are they? Why is the Temple empty?" "Your children have sinned," God explained. "They bowed to the idols of the world and have done violence unto one another. Therefore I have sent them into exile." "Perhaps," said Abraham, "they sinned in error, without realizing what they were doing. After all, they are but flesh and blood." "No," replied the Lord, "Israel has been a harlot who goes looking for sin. She has turned herself over completely to the flesh and has forgotten the image of the Holy Spirit in which she was created." "Then perhaps," Abraham persisted, "there were only a few who went astray, and not the many. Surely You would not punish the innocent with the guilty!" "I wish it were so," God answered. "but the harlot has committed lewd acts with many. Far too many." "And yet," Abraham continued, "You might have remembered the covenant of circumcision, as You did in the days of our enslavement in Egypt. Without Your memory of the covenant, their memory is like the wind." "But," God retorted, "They tried to forget the covenant with attempts to hide and undo their circumcision, in order to walk after the gods of the Gentiles." "Still Abraham would not be turned away." Perhaps if You had given them just a little more time, they would have repented and returned to You. After all, the sum of all time is Yours." "Am I to rejoice in their wickedness? God replied. "And you, Abraham, what joy can you find in this?" At that Abraham fell into despair, lowered his head into his hands, and wept bitterly. "O Lord of the Universe," he cried aloud, "Heaven forbid that they should be without hope!" At that moment a voice resounded from the very heights of the heavens, declaring, "The Lord has said that Israel is like a leafy

olive tree, fair and abounding in fruit!" Abraham understood and was com-
forted. Just as the olive tree produces it best fruit only at the end of the season, so
would Israel return from her exile and flourish at the end of time. Some say God
was comforted, too.

It is held within Judaism that the Messiah would rebuild the Temple. In
fact, Maimonides says this is how the Messiah will be recognized:

> *If a king will arise from the House of David who is learned in Torah and*
> *observant of the miztvot [commandments], as prescribed by the written*
> *law and the oral law, as David, his ancestor was, and will compel all of*
> *Israel to walk in [the way of Torah] and reinforce the breaches [in its ob-*
> *servance]; and fight the wars of God, we may, with assurance, consider*
> *him the Messiah… If he succeeds in the above, builds the temple in its*
> *place, and gathers the dispersed of Israel, he is definitely the Messiah.*[1]

Traditional Jews pray three times a day for the rebuilding of the temple
as well as praying for the Messiah to come. Malachi 3:1–5 speaks of
God's visitation and habitation of His temple, and Zechariah 6:9–15
speaks of "the Branch," Who will build the temple of the Lord, Who is a
priest which sits and rules on a throne.

There is also a spiritual temple that God is building in His people
(1Cor. 3:16–17; 1Pe. 2:4–5). The Hebrew Bible repeatedly promises God's
people that God would dwell and build a house within them (Lev. 26:12;
Jer. 32:38; Eze. 37:27; and 2Sa. 7:8,14). With the coming of the Messiah
into the world, all of God's people are indwelt by God's Holy Spirit. God
is building a spiritual temple in which both Jews and Gentiles turn to the
God of Israel through Yeshua the Messiah.

Even while the earthly Temple in Jerusalem was demolished, God
was building a redeemed worldwide spiritual temple. We also read of a
future day when the Messiah will set His feet on the mount of Olives
(Zec. 14:1–5) and bring cleansing to the land (Zec. 12:10–13:1), which will
bring about the building of the final temple.

In the book of Revelation, we see a heavenly city, the New Jerusalem, and the false city of Babylon, which is a perversion and counterfeit
of God's holy city. Revelation pictures a contrast between the New Jerusalem and the city of Babylon. The New Jerusalem is the chaste bride, the
wife of the Lamb (21:2,9); Babylon is the harlot, with whom the kings of
the earth fornicate (17:2). The glory of God and the nations walk in the
light of God's heavenly city (21:4); Babylon is full of corruption and de-
ceptions over the nations (17:2; 18:3,23; 19:2). The water of life and the
tree of life bring healing to the nations in God's city (21:6; 22:1–2); Baby-

lon's wine makes the nations drunk (14:8; 17:2; 18:3). God's people are called out of Babylon (18:4) and into the New Jerusalem (22:14).[2]

The New Jerusalem is Paradise restored (Isa. 11:9; 65:25). The beauty of the new creation is reflected in the all encompassing glory of God. As God makes "all things new," this new Jerusalem is like the 'Holy of Holies' in the temple described in 1 Kings 6:20. What we see in the book of Revelation is the history of both Israel and the church coming to fulfillment in the New Jerusalem.

The final restoration of the temple and the new city occurs when God comes and fully resides with man on earth (Rev. 21:3). Like God's glory and presence in the temple (Eze.43), this presence of God will be the fullness of His glory and holiness. All that is unholy is excluded from the holy city (Rev. 21:27). God's holiness and divine splendor fills the whole city. God is reviving, restoring, and making all things new (Isa. 65:17; Gal. 6:15; Rev. 21:5). These words are true and sure, for the Messiah has declared them.

❋ | *The* Victory *and the* Glory

Yom Kippur, the Day of Atonement, had just come to a close, when Rabbi Yitzchak Lurian, went to his disciple Rabbi Abraham Beruchim and declared, "Each Yom Kippur the names of those inscribed in the book of life for the coming year are revealed to me. Yours is not among them. Unless you do what is necessary to abolish the decree that has come forth from heaven, this will be your last year on earth." Hearing these words, Rabbi Abraham grew afraid and asked, "What must I do to avert the decree?" "You must leave for Jerusalem as soon as possible," Rabbi Yitzchak explained. "When you arrive in the city, go to the Western Wall, the last remnant of the holy Temple, and pour out your soul to God. If your prayers are worthy, you will have a vision of the Shekinah. That will be a sign that the decree has been suspended and your name had been inscribed in the Book of Life." Rabbi Abraham did just as he was told. After fasting for three days and three nights to purify himself for his prayers, he set out from Safed for the holy city. In order to further purify his soul, he chose not to go by donkey or wagon, but instead walked the whole way. By the time he reached the gates of Jerusalem, he felt as though he was floating on air. Once inside the city, he went straight to the Western Wall. As he approached the ancient stones that had heard so many prayers, his lips began to move in prayer. With every word he felt more and more as though his soul were about to leave his body and ascend to heaven. Just when he thought his soul would indeed depart, he saw an old woman dressed in black and deep in mourning emerge from the wall before him. "It is the shekinah!" the rabbi gasped to himself. "Oh, how she mourns over the destruction of her Temple and the exile of her children!" The shekinah walked toward him, drawing closer and closer, until she walked into him. Suddenly her sadness became his sadness. Suddenly he knew the unfathomable grief of a bride who has lost her groom, of a mother who has lost her child. He fell into a swoon and had a vision. In his vision he saw the shekinah once more, this time adorned in a robe of light, more brilliant than the sun at midday. Through the light that beamed from her face he could see the radiance of her joy. She reached out to him, cradled him in her arms, and whispered, "Do not despair, Abraham. My children will be returned to their homeland, and you will enjoy many blessings in the years to come." Rabbi Abraham awoke from his vision full of the joy of a renewed life and returned to Safed. There he went to Rabbi Yitzchak, who told him, "I see that you have been in the presence of the shekinah. I see, too, that you will have twenty-two more years of life, one for each letter of the Hebrew alphabet, from which the words of your prayers are made. For the light of the shekinah emanates from every letter — every letter is an avenue to the shekinah — and the shekinah has filled you with her light."

God is coming for a pure, spotless, and holy people. God is calling for Israel and the church to be a unified, holy, and spirit-directed community under the leadership of God's Messiah. When the glory of God comes, nothing will ever be the same. When the glory came the first time, it literally knocked the priests to the floor (1Ki. 8:10–11).

We have been living for too long in a time where *ichabod* ("the glory has departed") has been the exilic experience of God's people. The day is coming when *kabod* (the weight of God's presence) is coming so suddenly and powerfully that God will once again have a people like David — a people after God's own heart.

When God comes in the manifest fullness of His glory, everything and everyone will fall down in awe of Him. When the glory of God descended on earth at Pentecost, it brought fear among the community of God. The glory of God brought miracles, signs, and wonders, and many people were added to the church (Acts 5:11–16). God's glory will fill the whole earth (Isa. 6:3; Hab. 2:14).

God is looking for a broken and repentant people. God is looking for people who know the spiritual world is more real than the physical world. Oh, how we need a fresh revelation of the Father's love and a love for God's people Israel. Oh, how we need to know we are children of destiny, grafted into an eternal covenant with Israel. God is the only One Who can initiate revival and bring forth His glory.[1]

Man-centered plans and programs will never do this. A secret of God's Kingdom is that man's ways will fail, but God never fails. Paul says in 2 Timothy 2:11–13:

If we died with Him, we will also live with Him; if we endure, He will reign with Him; if we disown Him, He will disown us; if we are faithless, He will remain faithful, for He cannot disown Himself.

When it comes to the mystery of godliness, this mystery can seem great! Paul brings together the inter-relation of godliness with God's glory in and through an early church hymn that says:

> He appeared in a body, was vindicated by the Spirit, was seen by angels, was preached among the nations, was believed on in the world, was taken up in glory.[2]

The glory of the Messiah becomes the glory of the Christian community (2Cor. 3:17–18). As God brought forth light in creation, God is making us His new creation to fill our hearts with His light "to give us the light of the knowledge of the glory of God in the face of Christ" (2Cor. 4:6). We even carry the death of Jesus in our bodies, so that we may give His life away to others (4:12).

God is releasing His divine presence and glory to the nations.[3] People will see and sense things they have never seen or experienced before. God's mighty Word will go forth with such power that the whole world will be shaken. Prisons doors will be opened and the mighty will fall before the meek, who will inherit the earth. God's glory will bring such revelation and wisdom that even children will instruct those who have been trained in a world of adult instructors.

There will be deep, unspeakable secrets made known in seasons of divine encounter with God's people. God's eternal strategies and plans will make the wisdom of man seem foolish in comparison. Before the great "day of the Lord," there will be such a global conflict that only God's eternal decrees will stand. The last battle will be where God's victory shines forth against the night and there will be no more darkness, for the Lord's light will shine for everyone to see (Rev. 22:5).

Epilogue

❀ | Epilogue

When the hour of liberation was at hand for the Israelites of Egypt, our teacher Moses did not concern himself with the spoils of Egypt. No, instead of worrying about his own gain, he remembered his obligation to carry the bones of Joseph out of the land of bondage and into the land of promise. Although he did not know the secret of where Joseph's remains were buried, he recalled having heard it said that Serah, the daughter of Asher, knew. So he went to her and said, "Serah, the time of our liberation is at hand. Can you tell me where the coffin of our father Joseph lies buried, so that we may carry it with us to the Promise Land?" "Yes, I know," she answered. "but it will be impossible to retrieve it." "Why impossible?" "Because the Egyptians fashioned a coffin of iron for him," she explained, "and laid him in it. Then they took the coffin and placed it in the Nile, so that the waters that nourished their fields would be blessed. For they knew that Joseph brought many blessings to Egypt, and they wanted to keep him near forever. I am afraid that you will never be able to retrieve it from the river." Moses was not daunted by these words but immediately fetched several men to serve as bearers for Joseph's coffin and set out for the banks of the Nile. For he knew the power of the Most High to overcome all obstacles. When he reached the edge of the waters, Moses cried out, "Joseph, Joseph! The time for your liberation of your children has come, as the Holy One, blessed be He, promised it would when He declared, 'I shall deliver you.' Know that we have remembered the oath you imposed upon our fathers when you asked them to swear that they would take you out of this land and return you to the land of your birth. Therefore, show yourself, so that we may honor the oath. Otherwise we shall deem ourselves free of the promise our fathers made to you." No sooner did Moses finish speaking than the coffin of Joseph floated up to the surface of the waters and over to the bank where he and the bearers stood. They took it upon their shoulders and went to prepare for the liberation from Egypt. They carried it with them all the way to Mount Sinai. And from Mount Sinai they bore it, alongside the Ark of the Covenant that contained the tablets of the Torah, all the way to the Promise Land. Thus year after year, as the Israelites made their way through the wilderness, they took with them one ark containing the bones of Joseph and another containing the Shekinah, the divine presence of God. Each time they encountered travelers along the way, the strangers would ask them, "What is contained in these two arks that you bear?" The Israelites would reply, "One contains the bones of the dead, and the other is the vessel of the Shekinah." Is it your custom," they would ask further, "to bear the dead alongside the Shekinah?" "The one whose remains lie in this ark," the Israelites told them, "fulfilled all that is contained in the other." And so the wayfarers realized the wisdom of the Israelites. For the Israelites knew that, if their liberation was to be complete, they must bear with them the memory of the dead in their pursuit of the future.

If Israel and the church are to go forward, they must first go back. Understanding where one comes from and how that shapes one's identity must happen first before people go rushing into the unknown future.[1] God's story is to shape our story, and without knowing the details of that story, there is much to miss in the present. The church needs Israel, as Israel needs the church. The destinies of both are tied irrevocably together. Much Christian-Jewish dialogue on how to read and interpret the Hebrew Scriptures must be different, but how much more necessary for each to hear the other. Christians and Jews may find out they not only have a common story and history, but may begin remembering things lost to both traditions over time.[2]

Jews and Christians need to reexamine their respective roots, as well as their common history of exile and spiritual amnesia. God is calling both Israel and the Church to remember who they are and return once again to the common destiny God has for them.[3] It is even possible that God uses the mutual envy of Jews and Gentiles to, in the end, draw them together — both God and one another (Rom. 11:11).

The restoration of Israel will lead not only to the restoration of all the nations, but a renewed, unified people of God. The longing for God's presence, the suffering of God's people, and the wound of lost hopes and memories is coming to a close. God is waking His hardened-people, Israel, as well as His deaf and divided Church. The time of the Gentiles is almost over, as God is pouring out His spirit on all nations — especially those from the tribe of Abraham.

The history between Israel and the Church has too often been sad and unfortunate.[4] But, just as God did when His people grumbled in despair over the bitter waters at Marah, He is about to make it sweet (Exo. 17). Israel and the church are both messianic communities looking for the day when the Messiah will rule and bring peace, justice, and a completely new harmony to the whole creation.

Paul's vision of "one new man" in Christ was obscured early in the Church by the near total disappearance of Jews from the Christian church. The early church fathers seemed content to focus on Gentile conversions. The Church lost its vision of "the one new man in Christ," in Whom Jews and Gentiles will share the covenant and blessings of God.

Christian communities today are locked into so may cultural distortions and nationalistic captivities, so that even Gentiles are divided from each other and have abandoned their calling to provoke the Jews through holy communities.[5] The divine mandate that the church be unified with and within Israel is still in effect. The church of Jesus Christ needs to not only recover its Jewish roots, but even be willing to die for their older Jewish brother.[6]

The destiny of the world hinges on the Church's witness to and with Israel. The Christian tradition lived out in community needs to reclaim its historical continuity and relationship with Israel. The New Testament documents themselves are the product of a movement best described as a form of first-century Judaism. Oh, that all of God's people would have a prophetic and messianic vision, seeing God's purpose to finally establish His universal Kingdom in this world and the world to come. "*Maranatha*! Come, Lord Jesus, Come!" (Rev. 22:7,12,17,20; c.f. 1Cor. 16:22).

Endnotes

❀ | Endnotes

❀ | Preface (pp. 11–14)

1. For more on Restoration, the Stone-Campbell Movement, and the Cane Ridge Revival, see Leigh Eric Schmidt, *Holy Friars* (Eerdmans, 1989).

2. For the history of the first "unofficial" schism within Christianity, see Dan Finto, *Your People Shall Be My People* (Regal, 2001), and for a more scholarly treatment, see John Howard Yoder, *The Jewish-Christian Schism Revisited* (Eerdmans, 2003).

3. Hans Küng attempted to do this in his tome *Christianity: Essence, History, and Future* (Continuum, 2003).

❀ | Introduction (pp. 15–17)

1. Abraham Cohen, *Everyman's Talmud: The Major Teachings of the Rabbinic Sages* (BN Publishing, 2009) p. 61.

2. e.g., Psa. 67:1–3; 72:17–19; Isa. 45:22–23; 66:18; and Jer. 45–50, revealing both blessing and hope for even some of the nations who have been Israel's enemies.

3. See Isa. 66; Jer. 37; Amo. 9:11–15; Zep. 3; Zec. 14.

4. Tom Oden, *The Rebirth of Orthodoxy: Signs of New Life in Christianity* (Harper San Francisco, 2003) p. 18.

5. See Jesus' last words to His disciples in Acts 18, where He says, "…and you will be My witnesses in Jerusalem, and in all Judea, and Samaria, and to the ends of the earth."

6. A wonderful book that shows this is Henry Blackaby and Claude V. King, *Experiencing God: Knowing and Doing the Will of God* (Broadman & Holman, 1994).

THE GLORY OF ISRAEL'S STORY

❈ | *The* Glory *of* God (*pp. 20–23*)

1 Rabbai Rami Shapiro, *Hassidic Tales* (Skylight Paths, 2004), p. x.
2 Cohen, p. 9.
3 Ibid., p. 6.
4 God's providence is over everything; see Gen. 35:11–13; Deu. 10:13; 1Ch. 29:12; 2Ch. 20:6; Psa. 103:19; Isa. 40:21–26; Acts 17:24; Rom. 14:11–12; Eph. 1:20–22; Rev. 1:6; 19:6.
5 Cohen, pp. 8–9.

❈ | *The* Glory *of* Torah (*pp. 24–27*)

1 Jews call the Bible the Tanakh, and Christians call the Tanakh the Old Testament. I prefer to use the description "The Hebrew Bible."
2 Abraham Joshua Heschel, *Moral Grandeur and Spiritual Audacity: Essays Edited by Susannah Heschel*, (Ferrar, Straus, and Giroux, 1997), p. 196.
3 Cohen, p. 44.
4 Ibid., p. 45.
5 For an easy introduction to this topic, see Finto.
6 The most comprehensive description of the power and life of the Scripture in the experience of God's people is Psa. 119.

❈ | *The* Glory *of* Shema (*pp. 28–30*)

1 Michael L. Brown, *Answering Jewish Objections to Jesus: Vol. 2* (Baker, 2000), p. 8.

❈ | *The* Glory *of* Covenant (*pp. 31–33*)

1 Cohen, pp. 93–95.
2 See William Packer's *Narratives of a Vulnerable God* (Westminster/John Knox, 1994).
3 Scott Bader-Saye, *Church and Israel after Christendom* (Westview Press, 1999), p. 41.
4 Bader-Saye, p. 39.
5 Cohen, p. 21.

❈ | *The* Glory *of* Election (*pp. 34–36*)

1 Cohen, p. 60.
2 Ibid
3 Bader-Saye, p.31. For further study on the corporate view of election, see William Klein, *The New Chosen People* (Wipf & Stock, 2001).
4 Bader-Saye, p. 35.

❋ | *The* Glory *of* Israel (*pp. 37–39*)

[1] Yoder (2003) makes a convincing argument that the split and parting of the ways between Judaism and Christianity did not have to happen.

[2] Kenneth E. Bailey, *Jacob and the Prodigal: How Jesus Retold Israel's Story* (InterVarsity, 2003).

[3] Cohen, pp. 21–22.

[4] For an in-depth examination of the historical context, see Kenneth E. Bailey, *The Cross and the Prodigal: Luke 15 through the Eyes of Middle Eastern Peasants* (InterVarsity, 2005).

[5] I love it when Jews recognize the connection of Christian teachings to their Jewish faith, but I don't believe that when Jews confess faith in Christ, they cease to be Jews, nor do they have to give up synagogue worship. See, Mark Kinzer, *Post-Missionary Messianic Judaism: Redefining Christian Engagement with the Jewish People* (Brazos Press, 2005). Although I find many of Kinzer's conclusions provocative, I don't think one has to deny Jewish evangelism or witness when it comes to Christian Jews staying at home within their Jewish heritage and practices of Judaism.

[6] Cohen, pp. 354–55.

[7] This interesting phenomenon is spelled out in Peter Tsukahira's *God's Tsunami: Understanding Israel and End Time Prophecy* (Tsukahira, 2003).

[8] See Mark Ellingsen, *Reclaiming Our Roots* (Trinity Press International, 1999). This is one of the best histories of the Christian Church ever written, raising all the right questions for people doing historical theology and church history studies.

❋ | *The* Glory *of* Authority (*pp. 40–42*)

[1] Cohen, ch. 10, §. 1–11.

❋ | *The* Glory *of* Blessing (*pp. 43–45*)

[1] Reuben Hammer, *Entering Jewish Prayer* (Schoken Books, 1994), p. 161.

[2] For the history of both Jewish and Christian understandings of resurrection, see N.T. Wright, *The Resurrection of the Son of God* (Augsburg Fortress, 2003).

[3] Hammer, p. 164.

[4] Cohen, Ch. 7.

[5] See the Messiah's words in Mat. 25:31–46.

[6] For more on this point, see Brad H. Young, *Jesus the Jewish Theologian* (Hendrikson, 1995), Ch. 11.

[7] For a re-institution of Christians asking God personally for blessing, see Bruce Wilkinson, *The Prayer of Jabez* (Multnomah Press, 2000). It is a very standard Jewish practice for people to ask God to bless them.

❋ | *The* Glory *of* Grace (*pp. 46–48*)

[1] For a remarkable book on the grace of God, see Phillip Yancey, *What's So Amazing about Grace?* (Zondervan, 1997).

[2] Cohen, p. 17.

[3] Ibid., p. 17.

[4] Ibid., p. 20.

[5] Ibid., p. 18.

[6] Also see 2Pe. 3:9.

[7] Cohen, p. 18. "'The attribute of grace,' it was taught, 'exceeds that of punishment (i.e. justice) by five-hundred-fold.' The conclusion was deduced from the fact that in connection with punishment, God described Himself as 'visiting the iniquity of the fathers upon the children unto the third and fourth generation' (Exodus 20:5), but in connection with grace it is said, 'showing mercy unto the thousandth generation' (Exodus 20:6). The last phrase is, in the Hebrew, *alafim*, which is literally 'thousands' and must indicate at least two thousand. Grace, therefore, extends to at least two-thousand generations."

[8] Ibid., p. 79.

❋ | *The* Glory *of* Law (*pp. 49–51*)

[1] For further study on the Decalogue and the history of the Old Testament Law, see Frank Crusemann, *The Torah: Theology and Social History of the Old Testament Law* (Fortress Press, 1996).

[2] For preaching sensibly and sensitively in a Judeo-Christian context, see Marilyn J. Salmon, *Preaching Without Contempt: Overcoming Unintended Anti-Judaism* (Fortress Press, 2006).

[3] Cohen, p. 65. "The story is told that a heathen came to Shemmai with the request to be accepted as a convert on condition that he was taught the whole of the Torah while he stood on one foot. The Rabbi drove him away with the yard-stick which he was holding. He then went to Hillel with the same request; and he said to him, 'What is hateful to yourself, do not to your fellow-man. That is the whole of the Torah and the remainder is but commentary. Go learn it.'"

[4] See Mark Reasoner, *Romans in Full Circle* (Westminster/John Knox Press, 2005), Ch. 10.

[5] For a detailed study of the issues, see Marcus Bockmuehl, *Jewish Law in Gentile Churches* (Baker Books, 2000). Jesus' radicalness is rooted in His Nazarite vows of holiness, which took precedence at times over some Pharisaic interpretations of the Torah (especially see ch. 3 of his excellent study). The unity of God, Israel, and Torah are the foundation of Christian public and social ethics. It is not possible to remove Israel from Torah, nor can we replace Israel with Christianity. Both find their

completion in the Messiah, Who overcomes all divisions and even overcomes the world (John 16:33).

❀ | *The* Glory *of* Inheritance (*pp. 52–54*)

1   Finto (2001), pp. 117–18. "When the new state of Israel was established, the landmass consisted of 300 square miles. At the conclusion of the War of Independence in 1948, that had increased to 8,000 square miles. The Six-Days War of 1967 expanded her landmass to 26,000 square miles; the Yom Kippur War of 1973, to 36,000 square miles, though some of this has now been returned. But even this does not measure up to Israel's full inheritance as promised [by God to] both Abraham and Joshua (see Genesis 15:18 and Joshua 1:4)."

2   Israel's unbelief does not affect their fulfillment of biblical prophecy. God's Word clearly says that the promise of the land and final restoration as a Messianic people will be carried out (Rom. 3:3–4; 11:1–2).

3   For some New Testament examples, see Mat. 5:5; 19:29; Mark 10:17; Luke 10:25; 18:18; 1Cor. 6:9; Rev. 21:7.

4   In the last 30–35 years, over 400,000 of the first covenant people have come to believe in Jesus the Messiah. For more information on this and other points in this chapter, see Don Finto, *God's Promise and the Future of Israel* (Regal, 2006).

❀ | *The* Glory *of* Nations (*pp. 55–57*)

1   Cohen, pp. 63–4.

2   Ibid., p. 369. "Maimonides declared, 'The pious of the Gentiles will have a share in the World to Come.'"

3   Ibid., p. 66.

4   Ibid., p. 64.

5   Ibid., p. 253.

6   See Richard Bauckham, *The Climax of Prophecy* (T&T Clark, 1993), chapter 9.

7   There is a strong parallel between the nations that serve the Beast and the Lamb's conquest over the nations. There is numerical symbolism of seven (which stands for completeness) and the number four (which stands for the world). Therefore the number 28 becomes a significant number, where "the Lamb" is used 28 times throughout the book of Revelation. Therefore, the book of Revelation shows that the ultimate purpose of the Lamb's conquest is the conversion of all the nations of the world. We also see in Revelation that the Lamb has seven horns and there are Seven Eyes of the Seven Spirits of God sent out all over the world (5:6). There are four references to the Seven Spirits (1:4; 3:1; 4:5; 5:6) as the prophetic witness of the Church's purpose to win all the

nations back to true worship of the one true God.

THREADS OF DISASTER AND DELIVERANCE

✤ | *The* Dark Thread *of* Sin (*pp. 61–63*)

1 This prayer is from the Talmud. For one of the best contemporary discussions on the relevance of sin today, see Cornelius Pantenga, Jr., *Not the Way It's Supposed to Be: a Breviary of Sin* (Eerdman's, 1995).

2 Despite the diversity among rabbinic thought on controversial issues, like the Hereafter and the Fate of the Gentiles, the teachings of Yeshua and His followers are consistent with the rabbinic pattern.

3 Cohen, p. 95.

4 Ibid., p. 96.

5 Ibid.

6 Ibid., p. 97. The Talmud also says that lust is as the sin of adultery (p. 98; also see Jesus' teaching in Mat. 5:27–30).

7 Cohen, p. 98.

8 Ibid.

9 Ibid., p. 99.

10 Ibid., p. 100.

11 Ibid.

12 Ibid.

13 Ibid., p. 102.

14 The book of Revelation lists sins to avoid and remain faithful to the end, so that what is written in God's Word won't be blotted out (c.f., Rev. 3:5 with 20:15 and 21:27).

15 Cohen, p. 102.

16 Ibid., p. 103.

17 Ibid.

18 Ibid., p. 104.

19 Ibid.

✤ | *The* Bright Thread *of* Salvation (*pp. 64–66*)

1 N.T. Wright, *The New Testament and the People of God* (Fortress Press, 1992), pp. 335–38.

2 Also note the New Testament witness on this point: "The creation waits in eager expectation for the Sons of God to be revealed… in hope that creation itself will be liberated from its bondage and decay and brought into the glorious freedom of the Children of God" (Rom. 8:19, 20*b*).

❋ | *The* Dark Thread *of* Judgment (*pp. 67–69*)

1 Cohen, p. 110.

2 Ezekiel prophecies God's judgment upon Israel and 1Pe. 4:17 says: "...judgment begin with the House of God."

3 Cohen, p. 371.

4 Ibid.

5 Ibid, p. 372.

6 Ibid., p. 373.

7 Ibid., p. 373–4.

8 Ibid., p. 384. "The first class is alluded to in the text, 'Surely the righteous shall give thanks unto Thy name; the upright shall dwell in Thy presence.' ...The second is alluded to in, 'Blessed is the man whom Thou choosest and causest to approach that he may dwell in Thy courts.' ...The third is alluded to in, 'Blessed are they that dwell in Thy house.' ...The fourth is alluded to in, 'Lord, who shall sojourn in Thy tabernacle?' ...The fifth is alluded to in, 'Dwell in Thy holy hill.' ...The sixth is alluded to in, 'Who shall ascend into the Hill of the Lord?' ... And the seventh in, 'Who shall stand in His holy place?'"

9 Ibid., p. 375. There are many parallels to Jewish thoughts of heaven, like "The Book of Life" in Rev. 20:12, 15; 21:27; 22:18. In the Talmud, *Gan Eden* (Heaven) has at its center the "Tree of Life" (p. 388). Rev. 22:2 says, "Down the middle of the great street of the City... stood the Tree of Life..." and verse 19 says, "And if anyone takes words away from the book of prophecy, God will take away from him his share in the Tree of Life and in the Holy City (the New Jerusalem), which are described in this book. For rabbinic parallels in the book of Revelation on the New Jerusalem, see Bauckham, *The Theology of the Book of Revelation* (Cambridge University Press, 1993), ch. 6.

10 Ibid., p. 376.

11 Ibid., p. 381. "There is the teaching [in the Talmud], 'The fire of Gehinnon will never be extinguished, but it conflicts with the doctrine of the school of Hillel that Gehinnon will cease.'"

12 Ibid., p. 386.

13 For further study, see Bauckham, 1993.

❋ | *The* Bright Thread *of* Righteousness (*pp. 70–72*)

1 Cohen, p. 91. Jeremiah says that "the heart is deceitful above all things" (17:9), but Ezekiel prophesies that man will get a new heart (Eze. 18:31; 36:26).

2 Ibid., p. 188. The Messiah said it like this: "'Love the Lord your God with all your heart and with all your soul and with all your mind.' This is the first and greatest commandment and the second is like it: 'Love

your neighbor as yourself.' All the Law and the Prophets hang on these two commandments" (Mat. 22:37–40). First John also illustrates the rabbinic teaching: "If anyone says, 'I love God,' yet hates his brother, he is a liar. For anyone who does not love his brother, whom he has seen, cannot love God, Whom he has not seen. And he has given us this command: whoever loves God must also love his brother" (1Jo. 4:20–21).

THE DANCE OF FAITH

❋ | *The* Family Dance (*pp. 75–77*)
1 Cohen, p. 159.
2 Ibid.
3 Ibid., p. 160.
4 Ibid., p. 164.
5 Ibid., p. 182.
6 See the Messiah's words in Mat. 5:31–32; 19:3–12; Mark 10:2–12; Luke 16: 18–19.
7 Cohen, p. 167.
8 Ibid., p. 172.
9 Ibid., p. 173.
10 e.g., 1Ti. 5:8.

❋ | *The* Dance *of* Friendship (*pp. 78–80*)
1 e.g., Lev. 22:15; Deu. 10:18; 14:14–19,29; 24:17–22; 25:5–10; Psa. 18:5; 94:1–7; Isa. 1:16–17, 21–25; 10:2; Jer. 49:1.
2 Cohen, p. 184.
3 Ibid., p. 187.
4 Ibid., p. 205.

❋ | *The* Dance *of* Humility (*pp. 81–84*)
1 Cohen, p. 216.
2 Ibid.
3 Ibid., p. 217.
4 Mike Mason, *The Gospel According to Job* (Crossway, 1994), p. 338. This is one of the best "spiritual" commentaries ever written.
5 Heschel, *Moral Grandeur*, p. 391.

❋ | *The* Dance *of* Sacrifice (*pp. 85–87*)
1 Cohen, pp. 206–7, 355. "The Talmud teaches that in the hereafter in the New Temple, 'Sin having been abolished, there will be no need for expiatory sacrifices... in the hereafter, all offerings will cease, except the

thanksgiving offering, which will never come to an end."

2 Oskar Skarsaune, *In the Shadow of the Temple* (InterVarsity, 2002), p. 95.

3 The Hebrew people were saved from the Angel of Death by putting blood over the doorposts.

4 Whenever atonement is mentioned (49 times in all), it is always in connection with blood sacrifices (see Lev. 5:11–13). Lev. 17:11 says, "For the life of a creature is in the blood, and I have given it to you to make atonement for yourselves on the altar; it is the blood that makes atonement for one's life." Heb. 9:22 says it like this: "Without the shedding of blood, there is no forgiveness."

5 See Brown, *Vol. 2*, pp. 97*ff*.

6 Brown, *Vol. 2*, p. 155.

7 Ibid., p. 157; "The Messiah — the holy and righteous Servant of the Lord — was smitten for the sins of the world, and through His death we can receive atonement for our sins and healing for our souls."

8 For more on this point, see Brown, *Vol. 2*, pp. 155–67.

9 Possibly, there will only be thanksgiving offerings, or the animal sacrifices will serve as a kind of "memorial" to "the Lamb of God, Who takes away the sin of world" (John 1:29).

❈ | *The* Priest's Dance (*pp. 88–90*)

1 Deu. 31:9–13,26.

2 "I will hold you as a kingdom of priests and a consecrated nation" (Exo. 19:6).

3 Lev. 4:6, 17; 16:14–15.

4 Mal. 3:1–4. For more on this point, see Albert Vanhoye, *Old Testament Priests and the New Testament* (St. Bedes Publication, 1980), ch. 3.

5 See 2Sa. 7:12–16; Isa. 11:1–9; Jer. 33:15*ff*.

❈ | *The* Prophet's Dance (*pp. 91–93*)

1 Cohen, p. 45.

2 Ibid.

3 Ibid, p. 124.

4 Acts 2 fulfills this promise of the spirit of Jesus empowering the Church at Pentecost (c.f., Joe. 2:28).

5 Luke 4: 24–27; Mat. 13:57; Luke 13:33.

6 Acts 3:22, quoting Deu. 18:18.

7 The book of Revelation does distinguish between prophets and other Christians (11:18; 16:6; 18:20,24; 22:9), but the universality of Christian prophetic witness to the world is through the Church.

❀ | *The* King's Dance (*pp. 94–96*)

1 See Henri Nouwen's wonderful book, *Life of the Beloved* (Crossroad, 1995).

2 See Richard B. Hays, *Echoes of Scripture in the Letters of Paul* (Yale University Press, 1989), and *The Conversion of the Imagination: Paul as an Interpreter of Israel's Scripture* (Eerdamn's, 2005).

3 For an excellent study on this issue, see Vanhoye.

❀ | *The* Dance *of* Exile (*pp. 97–99*)

1 Cohen, pp. 59–60.

2 See Isa. 35:5 as well as 29:18*ff*; Mat. 11:2–5; and Luke 7:18–23.

❀ | *The* Sabbath Dance (*pp. 100–02*)

1 Cohen, p. 155.

1 Ibid., p. 223.

3 Samuel H. Drenser, ed., *I Asked for Wonder: A Spiritual Anthology Abraham Joshua Heschel* (Crossroad, 1986), p. 34.

4 The purpose of the Sabbath is given in Ezekiel's words: "I gave them My Sabbaths as a sign between us, so they would know that I the Lord made them holy. Every day is to be a holy day, even today" (Eze. 20: 12; see also Heb. 4).

5 Cohen, p. 156.

6 Ibid., pp. 155–56.

❀ | *The* Dance *of* Compassion (*pp. 103–05*)

1 Cohen, ch. 17.

2 Ibid., p. 226.

3 Ibid., pp. 231–2.

4 Cohen quotes this from the Talmud.

5 Ibid., p. 223.

6 e.g., Mat. 9:36; 14:14; 20:34; Mark 1:41; 6:34; 8:2; Luke 15:20.

❀ | *The* Dance *of* Fasting (*pp. 106–08*)

1 For the history of fasting in biblical times, see Elmer Towns, *Fasting for Spiritual Break-Through* (Regal, 1996) and for the practical and physical benefits of fasting, see Bill Bright, *The Coming Revival: America's Call to Fast, Pray, and "Seek God's Face"* (New Life Publications, 1995).

❀ | *The* Dance *of* Offering (*pp. 109–11*)

1 For more on this point, see Thomas E. Schmidt, *Hostility to Wealth in the Synoptic Gospels* (JSOT Press, 1987).

2 Cohen, p. 222.

³ For more information, see Craig Blomberg, *Neither Poverty Nor Riches* (Eerdmans, 1999). For a New Testament perspective, see Sandra Ely Wheeler, *Wealth as Peril and Obligation* (Eerdmans, 1995).

⁴ Blomberg, ch. 1.

⁵ When it comes to contemporary practices and understandings of the meaning of sacrifice, both Judaism and Christianity changed after the destruction of the Temple in 70 A.D. The blood of Christ is the complete fulfillment of all sacrifices. Even the animal sacrifices looked forward to the sacrificial Lamb of God (see Heb. 9–10).

⁶ Blomberg, ch. 8.

THE VICTORY OF GOD

❋ | *The* Victory *of* Prayer (*pp. 115–17*)

¹ Cohen, p. 82.

² Ibid, p. 367.

³ The Psalms have these musical notations. For two examples of structured musical acrostics, see Psa. 119 and Pro. 31.

⁴ John describes the sights and sounds in the book of Revelation like a roar of a lion, the sound of an ocean, or a sound like thunder.

❋ | *The* Victory *of* Angels (*pp. 118–20*)

¹ Cohen, p. 47. Also see 1Ki. 22:19; Isa. 6:1*ff*; Job 1:6.

² Ibid., p. 49.

² Ibid., p. 68.

⁴ Ibid., p. 49.

⁵ Ibid.

⁶ Ibid., p. 50.

⁷ Ibid., pp. 50–1.

⁸ Ibid., p. 55.

⁹ Ibid., p. 56.

¹⁰ Ibid., p. 57.

¹¹ See Rev. 19:10 and 22:9.

¹² See Richard Bauckham, *The Climax of Prophecy* (T&T Clark, 1993), ch. 4.

¹³ Doxologies to Christ also appear in 2Ti. 4:18; 2Pe. 3:18; and perhaps in 1Pe. 4:11 and Heb. 13:21.

❋ | *The* Victory *of* Worship (*pp. 121–23*)

¹ Some good studies on worship include Jack Hayford, *Worship His Majesty* (Word, 1987) and Ernest B. Gentile, *Worship God!* (Bible Temple Publishing, 1994).

² "Theology of Worship in the Old Testament," Yoshiaki Hattori, in

Worship: Adoration and Action, ed. D.A. Carson (Baker, 1993), p. 47. "Haggai 2:15–19 declares that when we are holy as God's people, we are able to receive God's blessing according to our work; but on the other hand, when we are unclean and are under God's judgment we are not able to receive God's blessing in spite of our hard work."

³ See Sally Morganthaler, *Worship Evangelism* (Zondervan, 1995).

❀ | *The* Victory *of* Community (*pp. 124–26*)

¹ Cohen, p. xxxvi.

² For more information, see Ellingsen, ch. 4.

³ See 1Ch. 16:15 and Psa. 105:8.

⁴ John 8:27–30.

⁵ 1Jo. 2:6.

❀ | *The* Victory *of* Peace (*pp. 127–29*)

¹ Cohen, pp. 203–4.

² Ibid., p. 204.

³ Ibid.

⁴ Ibid.

⁵ Ibid., p. 205.

⁶ Ibid., p. 253.

⁷ See C. Leonard Allen, *The Cruciform Church* (ACU Press, 1990).

⁸ Allen, p. 133. "First, through the cross we see the heart of God revealed most clearly. Second, only through the cross can we see the true nature of human sin and the depths of divine grace. And third, the cross provides the model for God's new social order, the Messianic community."

⁹ Stanley Hauerwas, *The Peaceable Kingdom* (University of Notre Dame, 1983), p. 107.

❀ | *The* Victory *of* Wisdom (*pp. 130–33*)

¹ Cohen, p. 141.

² Gen. 1:1 is often linked to Pro. 8:22 (also see Pro. 1:20–33; 3:13–26; 8:32–35; 9:4–6). Jewish tradition also identifies the three areas of Temple worship with the biblical wisdom tradition:

$$\text{Job} = \text{the outer Temple court}$$
$$\text{Ecclesiastes} = \text{the inner Temple court}$$
$$\text{Song of Songs} = \text{the Holy-of-Holies}$$

The Song of Songs therefore demonstrates a prophetic image for God's people of God's bridal and bridegroom message. I first heard this from

Mike Bickle, who has read almost every commentary on the Song of Songs.

3   For some New Testament examples, see 1Cor. 1:15–20; Heb. 1:2–3; Rev. 3:14; John 1:1–18. Michael Wyshogrod and Pinchas Lipide are two Jewish theologians who acknowledge that, historically and biblically, Jews have an incarnational aspect to their beliefs and practices. Many Orthodox Jews simply deny incarnational theology *contra* Christian claims without really looking into the matter. For more information, see Michael Wyshogrod, "A Jewish Perspective on Incarnation," *Modern Theology*, (12:2, April 1996), pp. 195–209.

4   Jesus spoke about being persecuted and losing one's life for His sake. Jesus even made demons depart by His own word of power. It was Him they feared! For more information, see Skarsaune, ch. 16.

❋ | *The* Messiah's Victory (*pp. 134–36*)

1   Cohen, p. 356.

2   Michael Brown, *Answering Jewish Objections: General and Historical Objections, Vol. 1* (Baker, 2000), p. 74. Also see his *Theological Objections, Vol. 2* (Baker, 2003), *Messianic Prophecy Objections, Vol. 3* (Baker 2003), *New Testament Objections, Vol. 4* (Baker, 2006), and *Traditional Jewish Objections, Vol. 5* (Purple Pomegranate Productions, 2010). This five-volume set is the best in-depth research on this topic done by a Messianic Jew.

3   It is interesting that the word *TaNaKH*, which is an acronym for *Torah* (Law of Moses), *Nevi'im* (Prophets), *Kethuvi'im* (Writings, the most prominent being the Psalms), reflects the same three-fold division of the Hebrew Scriptures. Until we read the Bible with more Jewish eyes, we will miss many of these connections, like the four-fold sense of Scripture from the ancient Eastern Orthodox and Roman Catholic Churches, whose roots are Jewish.

P'shat	=	the literal or plain-sense meaning of the text
Remez "hint"	=	the analogical meaning revealing related analogies and types
D'rash	=	the moral meaning and intertextual reading
Sod "secret"	=	the mystical, spiritual, and allegorical meaning of the text

4   The Temple was destroyed 46 years after the crucifixion of Jesus. I believe it is possible that the Temple was destroyed at this exact moment in history, when the news of Jesus' death and resurrection had been delivered to every Jew on the known earth. If the Temple would have

been destroyed earlier, that would have breached the Covenant between God and those Jews who had not yet heard the "good news." Conversely, if the Temple remained in place beyond that moment, Jesus' claims to be the fulfillment of the Temple would ring hollow or less true. It would also seem strange for God to allow a prophetic symbol of the literal Temple to continue when the thing it symbolized had actually come.

5 Brown, *Vol. 1*, p. 155. "Alfred Edersheim, the learned 19th century Jewish-Christian scholar, summarized the rabbinic data as follows: 'The passages in the Old Testament applied to the Messiah or to Messianic times in the most ancient Jewish writings… amount in all to 456, thus distributed: 75 from the Pentateuch, 243 from the Prophets, 138 from the Haggiographa, and supported by more than 558 separate quotations from rabbinic writings… the rabbinic references might have been considerably increased, but it seemed useless to quote the same application of a passage in many different books.'"

6 See King David's words in Psa. 16. For the most detailed and comprehensive work on the resurrection of Jesus, see N.T. Wright's massive tome, *The Resurrection of the Son of God* (Fortress, 2003).

7 Mal. 3 says that the final atonement for Israel's sins had to be made before the Second Temple was destroyed (also see Dan. 9:24–27). For works dealing with the deity of the Messiah, see Richard Bauckham, *God Crucified: Monotheism & Christology in the New Testament* (Eerdmans, 1998); Oscar Skarsune, *In the Shadow of the Temple: Jewish Influences on Early Christianity* (InterVarsity, 2002), esp. ch. 16; and N.T. Wright, *The Challenge of Jesus* (InterVarsity, 1999), esp. ch. 5.

❀ | *The* Victory *of the* Kingdom (*pp. 137–39*)

1 Cohen, p. 4.

2 Ibid., p. 212; For a New Testament perspective, see Richard Hays, *The Moral Vision of the New Testament* (Harper San Francisco, 1996).

3 Ibid., p. 239.

4 Ibid.

5 God's Kingdom is right-side-up, but seems up-side-down in our twisted, fallen world. For an important study on this topic, see Donald B. Kraybill, *The Upside-Down Kingdom* (Herald Press, 1978).

6 There are over 80 references to the Kingdom in the Gospels. Jesus told stories about the Kingdom (see Mat. 13). Jesus established a Messianic community, where His death and resurrection defeated the kingdom of evil and brought the age of the Kingdom of God.

7 For more information, see Howard A. Snyder, *The Community of the King* (InterVarsity, 1977).

8 The Church so accommodates and is subverted by the values of the culture today that the Church needs Israel as a model to be a counter-cultural, visible witness to the world at-large.

9 Phillip Yancey, *The Jesus I Never Knew* (Zondervan, 1995).

10 For further study Mortimer Arias, *Announcing the Reign of God* (Fortress Press, 1984).

11 Yancey, p. 183.

❋ I *The* Victory *of the* Spirit (*pp. 140–42*)

1 Cohen, pp. 124–5.

2 See Isa. 48:16; Eph. 4:4–6; 1Pe. 1:2; 2Cor. 13:14; John 14:16–23; 15:26.

3 Eze. 37:14, "I will put My Spirit in you and you will live..."

4 Skarsaune, p. 351.

❋ I *The* Victory *of* Faith (*pp. 143–45*)

1 Heschel, *Moral Grandeur*, § 5 on faith.

2 For more information, see Daniel Taylor's excellent book *The Myth of Certainty* (Zondervan, 1986).

3 Cohen, p. 79.

4 For the relationship between faith and works, see John F. MacArthur, Jr.'s pointed discussion in *The Gospel According to Jesus* (Zondervan, 1988).

5 MacArthur, p. 252.

❋ I *The* Victory *of* Restoration (*pp. 146–48*)

1 Brown, *Vol, 2*, p. 170.

2 For more information, see Bauckham, *Theology*, ch. 6.

❋ I *The* Victory *and the* Glory (*pp. 149–51*)

1 For the history of revivals, see Wesley Duewel, *Revival Fire* (Zondervan, 1995). For practical, personal, and corporate responses, see Michael L. Brown, *Holy Fire* (ICN Ministries, 1996).

2 1Ti. 3:16.

3 For a fascinating study of this phenomenon, see Phillip Jenkins, *The Next Christendom: the Coming of Global Christianity* (Oxford, 2002).

EPILOGUE (*pp. 155–57*)

1 God's people must prophetically confront the present with God's final end in mind. For more on this point, see Os Guiness, *Prophetic Untimeliness* (Baker, 2003).

2 An example of Jewish apocalyptic tradition that Christians need to dis-

cern and understand are the three volumes of the Book of Enoch, which are part of the Pseudopigrapha (a collection of Jewish religious writings from the years 200 BC to 200 BCE/AD.).

3 See Ephraim Radner's two excellent works: *The End of the Church* (Eerdamns, 1998) and *Hope among the Fragments* (Brazos Press, 2004).

4 See Michael L. Brown, *Our Hands Are Stained with Blood* (ICN Ministries, 1992).

5 The Church must resist the deification of military, political, and economic prosperity. The Church must purify herself from all worldly compromises and idolatry.

6 The Church's witness will only have value if it knows truth worth dying for.